IN THE KITCHEN WITH Mary & Martha Cookin' Up Christmas

D1469271

A Cookbook to Make Your
Christmas a Little Merrier

BARBOUR
PUBLISHING

*Special thanks to Darcie Anzalone for her help
in compiling these delicious holiday dishes!*

Cover Design: Greg Jackson, Thinkpen Design, LLC
Cover Illustration: Karen M. Reilly

Published by Barbour Publishing, Inc., P.O. Box 719, Uhrichsville, Ohio 44683
www.barbourbooks.com

Our mission is to publish and distribute inspirational products offering exceptional value and biblical encouragement to the masses.

Printed in China.

Member of the
Evangelical Christian
Publishers Association

5 4 3 2 1

Dedication

To Shelly,
Thank you for giving me two of the most
precious gifts I'll ever receive in my lifetime.
Mary

To our Lord and Savior,
Thank You for the first and best Christmas gift.
Martha

A Special Message from Mary & Martha

Hi! Mary and Martha here. We're delighted to have you join us for *Cookin' Up Christmas*!
We've got oodles of festive ideas for you this season—including only the best holiday recipes, from appetizers to desserts and everything in between. Whether you're preparing a small feast for your family or gearing up to host a spectacular  Christmas celebration, we've got you covered. Your family and guests will give rave reviews as you wow them with your culinary creations.

In addition to dozens of recipes guaranteed to get you ready for the season, we'll be making appearances throughout this book with some down-home old-fashioned inspiration and helpful tips to make your holiday a little merrier—and more meaningful. So be on the lookout, and. . . Happy holiday cooking!

MARY & MARTHA

Dear Lord,
Help me to keep my eyes fixed on You
throughout the Christmas season. When the
commercialism of the holiday threatens to
snuff out the real meaning of Christmas in my
heart, remind me of the Gift of Hope You sent
on that silent night so long ago.
Amen.

CONTENTS

STARTIN' THE HOLIDAY OFF RIGHT

Appetizers and Finger Foods for Your Festivities

Small cheer and great welcome make a merry feast.

WILLIAM SHAKESPEARE (1564–1616), English poet and playwright

Bacon and Tomato Dip

½ POUND BACON

3 SMALL TOMATOES, QUARTERED AND SEEDED

1 (8 OUNCE) PACKAGE CREAM CHEESE, SOFTENED

3 TEASPOONS PREPARED MUSTARD

¼ TEASPOON HOT SAUCE

1½ CUPS ALMONDS

3 TABLESPOONS MINCED GREEN ONIONS

In a large skillet, fry bacon until crisp. Drain, crumble, and set aside. In food processor basket, combine tomatoes, cream cheese, mustard, and hot sauce. Add the almonds, onions, and bacon. Blend until almonds are chopped. Refrigerate at least 2 hours to blend flavors. Serve with crackers or vegetables.
Yield: 10 to 12 servings

Bacon Cheddar Spread

1½ CUPS SHREDDED MILD CHEDDAR CHEESE

4 OUNCES CREAM CHEESE, SOFTENED

3 TABLESPOONS MINCED GREEN ONIONS

3 TABLESPOONS MAYONNAISE

2 TEASPOONS PREPARED MUSTARD

½ TEASPOON WORCESTERSHIRE SAUCE

10 SLICES BACON, COOKED AND CRUMBLED

Combine all ingredients in a medium mixing bowl until smooth. Chill to blend flavors. Serve with crackers.
Yield: 6 to 10 servings

Give an anonymous gift to someone in need.
A gift certificate for groceries, toys, a donation
of money—the possibilities are endless.
Let God receive all the praise and honor
for your thoughtfulness.

"Let your light shine before men, that they may. . .praise your Father in heaven."
MATTHEW 5:16

Bacon-Topped Cheese Ball

1 (8 OUNCE) PACKAGE CREAM CHEESE, SOFTENED

1½ CUPS SOUR CREAM

2 CUPS (8 OUNCES) SHREDDED SWISS CHEESE

2 CUPS (8 OUNCES) SHREDDED SHARP CHEDDAR CHEESE

3 TABLESPOONS GRATED ONION

3 TABLESPOONS SWEET PICKLE RELISH

1 TABLESPOON PREPARED HORSERADISH

¼ TEASPOON SALT

¼ TEASPOON LEMON-PEPPER SEASONING

⅛ TEASPOON GARLIC POWDER

6 SLICES BACON, COOKED AND FINELY CRUMBLED

¼ CUP CHOPPED FRESH PARSLEY

¼ CUP ALMONDS, TOASTED AND FINELY CHOPPED

Beat together cream cheese and sour cream in a large mixing bowl until
smooth. Add shredded cheeses, onion, pickle relish, horseradish, salt,
lemon-pepper seasoning, and garlic powder; beat on low speed until well
blended. Cover and chill thoroughly.

Combine bacon, parsley, and almonds; stir well. Shape chilled cheese
mixture into a ball; roll in bacon mixture, pressing bacon mixture into
cheese ball with hands. Wrap cheese ball tightly in waxed paper; chill until
ready to serve. Serve with assorted crackers.

Yield: one 6-inch cheese ball

Baked Water Chestnuts

1 CAN WHOLE WATER CHESTNUTS

½ CUP SOY SAUCE

SUGAR

4 SLICES BACON, CUT IN HALF LENGTHWISE AND WIDTHWISE

Drain water chestnuts. Marinate in soy sauce for 30 minutes. Drain sauce
from water chestnuts and roll each water chestnut in sugar. Wrap each
chestnut in strip of bacon. Bake at 400° for 30 minutes.
Yield: 8 servings

Blue Cheese-Stuffed Dates

2 OUNCES BLUE CHEESE

MILK

12 DRIED DATES, PITTED AND CUT IN HALF LENGTHWISE

24 BLANCHED ALMONDS, TOASTED

CAYENNE PEPPER

In a small bowl, mix the cheese with hand mixer until creamy. Add a few drops of milk if cheese is too crumbly. Place the dates on a serving platter. Spread about 1 teaspoon of cheese on the cut side of each date. Top with 1 almond. Sprinkle stuffed dates with a dash of cayenne pepper. Serve. Yield: 6 to 8 servings

Bruschetta

4 CUPS ROMA TOMATOES, CHOPPED AND SEEDED

1 MEDIUM ONION, CHOPPED

6 TO 8 BASIL LEAVES, CHOPPED

2 TO 3 TABLESPOONS FRESH OREGANO, CHOPPED

3 TO 5 GARLIC CLOVES, MINCED

½ TEASPOON BLACK PEPPER

2 TABLESPOONS OLIVE OIL

1 (16 OUNCE) LOAF FRENCH BREAD, CUT INTO 24 SLICES

OLIVE OIL COOKING SPRAY

In a medium mixing bowl, combine tomatoes, onion, basil, oregano, garlic, black pepper, and olive oil. Cover and chill for 2 to 3 hours to blend flavors.
   When ready to serve, spray each bread slice with cooking spray and broil until lightly browned. Spoon mixture onto bread slices and serve.
Yield: 24 slices

Cheese and Chicken Empanadas

½ CUP SHREDDED MONTEREY JACK CHEESE

½ CUP SHREDDED MILD CHEDDAR CHEESE

1 CUP SHREDDED COOKED CHICKEN

1 JALAPEÑO PEPPER, DICED

½ TABLESPOON MINCED RED ONION

½ TEASPOON GROUND CUMIN

½ TEASPOON SALT

2 FROZEN PIE SHELLS, THAWED

3 EGG YOLKS, LIGHTLY BEATEN

2 TABLESPOONS COARSE KOSHER SALT

1 TABLESPOON CHILI POWDER

In a bowl, mix together cheeses, chicken, jalapeño, onion, cumin, and salt. Refrigerate until ready to assemble empanadas.

On a floured surface, roll out pie shells and cut into eight 4-inch circles. Use all the dough by rerolling scraps. Place approximately 2 tablespoons of cheese and chicken mixture in center of each dough circle. Fold each circle in half and crimp edges with a fork. Place on a greased baking pan or cookie sheet and brush top of each empanada with egg yolk. Sprinkle top with kosher salt and chili powder. Bake at 400° for 12 to 13 minutes. Serve warm or at room temperature.

Yield: 8 servings

To keep dough from sticking to your rolling pin, try using nylon. Take a clean, never-worn knee-high stocking and cut off the toe. Slide the nylon over your rolling pin. The nylon helps hold an even layer of flour on the pin so you can easily flatten moist dough.

Cheese Straws

½ CUP BUTTER, SOFTENED

1 POUND SHREDDED SHARP CHEDDAR CHEESE

½ TEASPOON SALT

1¾ CUPS FLOUR

¼ TEASPOON GROUND RED PEPPER

In a large bowl, cream butter. Add remaining ingredients and combine thoroughly. On a floured surface, roll into ¼-inch-thick rectangle. Cut into narrow strips approximately 4 inches long. Bake at 350° for 20 to 25 minutes.
Yield: 30 to 40 straws

Tired of your Christmas ornament collection? Mix it up this year! Purchase kitchen-themed decorations for the holidays. Pick out inexpensive small kitchen gadgets at your local dollar store. Attach them to your tree with gingham ribbon—or with ribbon that coordinates with your other decorations—for a unique look.

Cinnamon-Glazed Almonds

1 EGG WHITE

1 TEASPOON COLD WATER

4 CUPS WHOLE ALMONDS

½ CUP SUGAR

¼ TEASPOON SALT

½ TEASPOON GROUND CINNAMON

Lightly grease a 10 x 15-inch jelly roll pan. Lightly beat the egg white; add water, and beat until frothy but not stiff. Place almonds in a large bowl. Drizzle egg mixture over nuts and stir until well coated. In a small bowl, combine sugar, salt, and cinnamon; sprinkle over nuts. Toss to coat, and spread evenly in the prepared pan. Bake at 250° for 45 minutes to 1 hour, stirring occasionally, until golden. Allow to cool completely. Store almonds in an airtight container.
Yield: 4 cups

Corned Beef Dip

1 (12 OUNCE) CAN CORNED BEEF

1 (5 OUNCE) JAR PREPARED HORSERADISH

1 CUP MAYONNAISE

1 MEDIUM ONION, MINCED

BLACK PEPPER TO TASTE

WORCESTERSHIRE SAUCE TO TASTE

PARTY RYE BREAD OR CRACKERS

Chop the corned beef finely. In a mixing bowl, combine the beef with horseradish, mayonnaise, onion, pepper, and Worcestershire sauce. Chill for at least 3 to 4 hours to blend flavors. Spoon into a serving bowl and serve with party rye or crackers.
Yield: 3 cups

To keep your dips chilled at a long party, choose two complementary glass bowls— one larger than the other. Fill the larger bowl with ice chips. Fill the smaller bowl with your dip and set the bowl down into the ice.

Cranberry Salsa

1 CUP WATER

1 CUP SUGAR

1 (12 OUNCE) PACKAGE FRESH OR FROZEN CRANBERRIES

2 TABLESPOONS CHOPPED, CANNED JALAPEÑO PEPPERS

1 TEASPOON DRIED CILANTRO

¼ TEASPOON GROUND CUMIN

1 GREEN ONION, THINLY SLICED

1 TEASPOON LIME JUICE

In a saucepan, bring water and sugar to a boil over medium heat. Add cranberries; return to boil. Gently boil cranberries for 10 minutes without stirring. Pour into a glass mixing bowl. Gently stir in remaining ingredients. Place a piece of plastic wrap directly on salsa. Cool to room temperature, then refrigerate. Serve with tortilla chips.
Yield: 3 cups

Creamy Cinnamon Fruit Dip

1 (8 OUNCE) CARTON SOUR CREAM

1½ TEASPOONS GROUND CINNAMON

1 (13 OUNCE) JAR MARSHMALLOW CREAM

Blend all ingredients together until creamy. Chill. Serve with fresh fruit.
Yield: 3 cups

A "real" fruit bowl makes a fanciful holiday serving dish for your fruit dip. Cut a whole fresh pineapple lengthwise—leaving the top green on. Hollow out the fruit, leaving a thick wall. Fill the bowl with dip. Other rind fruits, such as oranges, lemons, and cantaloupe, also make good serving bowls.

Debbie's Cheese Ball

1 JAR OLD ENGLISH CHEESE SPREAD

1 JAR ROKA BLUE CHEESE SPREAD

1 (8 OUNCE) PACKAGE CREAM CHEESE, SOFTENED

1 SMALL ONION, MINCED

1 DASH WORCESTERSHIRE SAUCE

¾ CUP CHOPPED PECANS

With a fork, thoroughly blend cheese spreads, cream cheese, onion, and Worcestershire sauce. Sprinkle chopped pecans onto a sheet of waxed paper. Spoon cheese mixture onto pecans. Roll cheese mixture in pecans and form into a ball. Wrap ball in plastic wrap and chill thoroughly before serving with crackers.
Yield: 12 to 15 servings

For a fun twist, create a pinecone out of your cheese ball. Shape your cheese mixture into a cone. Use whole or sliced almonds to cover the cheese ball in overlapping rows like the rows on a pinecone.

Ham Bites

1 CUP DRY BREAD CRUMBS, DIVIDED

1 CUP GROUND COOKED HAM

2 EGGS, BEATEN

1½ CUPS (2 OUNCES) SHREDDED SHARP CHEDDAR CHEESE

¼ CUP GRATED ONION

2 TABLESPOONS BROWN SUGAR

1 TABLESPOON DIJON MUSTARD

VEGETABLE OIL

Combine ½ cup bread crumbs with all of the ground ham, eggs, shredded cheese, onion, brown sugar, and mustard in a large bowl. Mix well. Form ham mixture into 1-inch balls. Roll balls in remaining ½ cup bread crumbs, pressing firmly so that crumbs adhere. Cover and refrigerate ham balls until chilled thoroughly.

Heat vegetable oil to 375° and deep-fry ham balls for 1 to 2 minutes or until golden brown. Drain on paper towels. Serve immediately with barbecue sauce, honey mustard, or other favorite dipping sauces.
Yield: 30 appetizers

Holiday Cheese Ring

4 CUPS SHREDDED SHARP CHEDDAR CHEESE

1 CUP FINELY CHOPPED PECANS

1 CUP MAYONNAISE

1 SMALL ONION, FINELY CHOPPED

1 PINCH BLACK PEPPER

1 PINCH CAYENNE PEPPER

1 DASH WORCESTERSHIRE SAUCE

1 JAR STRAWBERRY OR RASPBERRY PRESERVES

In a mixing bowl, blend together all ingredients except preserves. Spoon mixture into a greased gelatin ring mold. Refrigerate for 3 to 4 hours. Transfer the cheese ring from the mold to a serving plate. Spoon preserves into the center of the ring. Serve with crackers.
Yield: 12 to 15 servings

Send a Christmas newsletter to your family and friends. Update them on the latest news and happenings, and add a scripture verse and other inspiring thoughts you may want to share. Be sure to include one of your favorite holiday recipes!

Hot Crab Dip

1 (8 OUNCE) PACKAGE CREAM CHEESE, SOFTENED

½ TEASPOON PREPARED HORSERADISH

2 TABLESPOONS MINCED GREEN ONIONS

1 TABLESPOON WORCESTERSHIRE SAUCE

1 (6½ OUNCE) CAN CRABMEAT, DRAINED

⅓ CUP SLIVERED ALMONDS

PAPRIKA

In a mixing bowl, blend together cream cheese, horseradish, onions, Worcestershire sauce, and crabmeat. Spread into a 3-cup baking dish. Sprinkle with almonds, then with paprika. Bake at 350° for 30 minutes. Serve with wheat or rye crackers.
Yield: 8 servings

Hot Ryes

1 CUP FINELY GRATED SWISS CHEESE

¼ CUP COOKED AND CRUMBLED BACON

1 (4½ OUNCE) CAN CHOPPED BLACK OLIVES

¼ CUP MINCED ONION

1 TEASPOON WORCESTERSHIRE SAUCE

¼ CUP MAYONNAISE

1 LOAF PARTY RYE BREAD

Mix first six ingredients together. Spread 2 to 3 teaspoons of mixture on each slice of bread. Bake at 375° for 10 to 15 minutes or until bubbly. Yield: 2½ dozen appetizers

Marinated Cheese

½ CUP OLIVE OIL

½ CUP WHITE WINE VINEGAR

1 (2 OUNCE) JAR DICED PIMIENTO, DRAINED

3 TABLESPOONS CHOPPED FRESH PARSLEY

3 TABLESPOONS MINCED GREEN ONIONS

3 GARLIC CLOVES, MINCED

1 TEASPOON SUGAR

¾ TEASPOON DRIED WHOLE BASIL

½ TEASPOON SALT

½ TEASPOON FRESHLY GROUND BLACK PEPPER

1 (8 OUNCE) BLOCK SHARP CHEDDAR CHEESE, CHILLED

1 (8 OUNCE) PACKAGE CREAM CHEESE, CHILLED

FRESH PARSLEY (OPTIONAL)

Combine first ten ingredients in a jar; cover tightly and shake vigorously. Set marinade aside. Cut block of cheddar cheese in half lengthwise. Cut crosswise into ¼-inch-thick slices; set aside. Repeat procedure with cream cheese. Arrange cheese slices, alternating between cheddar and cream cheese, in a shallow baking dish, standing slices on edge. Pour marinade over cheese slices. Cover and marinate in refrigerator at least 8 hours.

Transfer cheese slices to a serving platter in the same alternating fashion, reserving marinade. Spoon marinade over cheese slices. Garnish with fresh parsley sprigs if desired. Serve with assorted crackers. Yield: 16 servings

Party Meatballs

½ POUND GROUND BEEF

⅓ CUP LEMON-LIME SODA

½ CUP ITALIAN BREAD CRUMBS

1 EGG, BEATEN

½ TEASPOON GARLIC SALT

½ TEASPOON ONION SALT

18 STUFFED GREEN OLIVES

In a medium bowl, combine ground beef, lemon-lime soda, bread crumbs, egg, garlic salt, and onion salt. Mix well. Form a small amount of mixture into a ball around a stuffed green olive. Repeat with remaining mixture. Place under broiler for about 10 minutes or until browned.
Yield: 18 meatballs

Piglets-in-a-Blanket

1 (10 COUNT) CAN REFRIGERATOR BISCUITS

20 COCKTAIL SAUSAGES

Cut each biscuit in half and wrap each half around a sausage. Place on an ungreased cookie sheet and bake at 400° for 8 to 10 minutes or until biscuits are lightly browned. Serve with favorite dipping sauces.
Yield: 20 appetizers

Pick up some great gifts this holiday season for your loved ones who enjoy cookin' up tasty treats. Measuring spoons and cups, spices, recipe cards, a recipe organizer, dish towels, and other fun kitchen gadgets are sure to please the family chef.

Ravioli Bites

2 TABLESPOONS MILK

1 EGG, LIGHTLY BEATEN

1 CUP ITALIAN BREAD CRUMBS

1 (25 OUNCE) PACKAGE FROZEN CHEESE-FILLED RAVIOLI

OLIVE OIL COOKING SPRAY

2 TABLESPOONS GRATED PARMESAN CHEESE

1 CUP SPAGHETTI SAUCE

Combine milk and egg in a small bowl. Place bread crumbs in another shallow bowl. Dip each ravioli in milk mixture, then coat with bread crumbs. Place on baking sheet. Spray each ravioli liberally with cooking spray; recoat with bread crumbs and spray a second time with cooking spray. Bake at 450° for 8 to 10 minutes or until golden brown. Sprinkle with Parmesan cheese and serve with spaghetti sauce.
Yield: 9 servings

Sausage and Apple Bites

2½ CUPS BAKING MIX

1 POUND MILD BREAKFAST SAUSAGE

1½ CUPS SHREDDED SHARP CHEDDAR CHEESE

¼ CUP FINELY CHOPPED CELERY

2 TABLESPOONS MINCED ONION

1 PINCH GARLIC POWDER

2 MEDIUM TART APPLES, FINELY CHOPPED

In a mixing bowl, combine all ingredients; knead until well blended. Roll into 1-inch balls and place on a greased cookie sheet. Bake at 350° for 15 to 20 minutes or until browned, turning each ball after 10 minutes. Yield: 36 appetizers

Spicy Cheese Popcorn

8 CUPS POPPED POPCORN

2 TABLESPOONS BUTTER, MELTED

½ TEASPOON CHILI POWDER

¼ TEASPOON GARLIC POWDER

¼ TEASPOON ONION POWDER

¼ CUP GRATED PARMESAN CHEESE

SALT TO TASTE

Place popped popcorn in a large mixing bowl. In a seperate bowl, combine butter, chili powder, garlic powder, and onion powder; pour mixture over popcorn, stirring to coat. Sprinkle with Parmesan cheese and salt; toss to coat.
Yield: 8 cups

The Christmas edibles aren't only for the table. The tree is also a great place to display your kitchen creations. Make garland that can be snacked on. Try a variety of treats, such as nuts, popcorn, dried fruit, marshmallows, gum drops, wrapped candies, and the like.

Spinach Phyllo Triangles

1 (10 OUNCE) PACKAGE FROZEN
CHOPPED SPINACH, THAWED

1/3 CUP MINCED ONION

2 TABLESPOONS BUTTER OR
MARGARINE, MELTED

1 CUP GRATED PARMESAN CHEESE

3/4 CUP (3 OUNCES) SHREDDED
SHARP CHEDDAR CHEESE

1 EGG, BEATEN

3 TABLESPOONS SOFT BREAD
CRUMBS

1/2 TEASPOON GARLIC POWDER

1/4 TEASPOON CAYENNE PEPPER

1/4 TEASPOON SALT

1 DASH HOT SAUCE

1/2 (16 OUNCE) PACKAGE FROZEN
PHYLLO PASTRY, THAWED

1 CUP BUTTER OR MARGARINE,
MELTED AND DIVIDED

PAPRIKA

Drain thawed spinach well, pressing between paper towels until barely moist. Sauté onion in 2 tablespoons butter until tender. Add spinach, Parmesan and cheddar cheeses, egg, bread crumbs, garlic powder, cayenne pepper, salt, and hot sauce. Stir well.

Cut sheets of phyllo lengthwise into forty-two 3-inch strips. Working with one strip at a time, brush each strip lightly with melted butter. Keep remaining strips covered. Place 2 teaspoons spinach mixture at base of phyllo strip; fold the right bottom corner over to form a triangle. Continue folding back and forth into a triangle to end of strip. Repeat procedure with remaining phyllo strips, melted butter, and spinach mixture.

Place triangles, seam side down, on ungreased baking sheets. Brush tops lightly with remaining melted butter. Bake at 325° for 30 to 35 minutes. Drain on paper towels. Sprinkle triangles with paprika.
Yield: 3½ dozen appetizers

Stuffed Mushrooms

12 MEDIUM FRESH MUSHROOMS

2 TABLESPOONS BUTTER OR MARGARINE, DIVIDED

¼ CUP FINELY CHOPPED GREEN PEPPER

¼ CUP FINELY CHOPPED CELERY

¼ CUP FINELY CHOPPED ONION

SALT AND PEPPER TO TASTE

Wipe mushrooms with damp cloth to clean. Remove stems and chop stems finely. Melt 1 tablespoon butter in skillet. Sauté mushroom caps on bottom side only for 2 to 3 minutes. Remove from skillet and arrange, round side down, in shallow baking dish. Sauté stems, green pepper, celery, and onion in remaining butter until tender, about 4 to 5 minutes. Season with salt and pepper. Spoon mixture into mushroom caps. Bake at 350° for 15 minutes or until heated through.
Yield: 6 servings

Share God's love with others this Christmas. Volunteer your time—or your talents—to a worthy cause. You may never know the impact you have on others. After all, kindness is contagious!

*Whatever you do, whether in word or deed,
do it all in the name of the Lord Jesus.*
COLOSSIANS 3:17

White Chocolate–Coated Party Mix

½ (20 OUNCE) BOX TOASTED OATS CEREAL

½ (12 OUNCE) BOX RICE SQUARES CEREAL

½ (16 OUNCE) BOX WHEAT SQUARES CEREAL

½ (9 OUNCE) BAG SMALL UNSALTED PRETZELS

2 TO 3 POUNDS WHITE CHOCOLATE DISKS

1 (21.3 OUNCE) BAG GREEN AND RED CANDY-COATED CHOCOLATE PIECES

In a large mixing bowl, combine cereals and pretzels. Set aside. In a microwave-safe dish, melt the white chocolate according to package directions. Pour melted chocolate over cereal and stir to coat. Sprinkle chocolate pieces over mixture and gently stir to combine. Line cookie sheet with waxed paper. Spread mixture on sheet and allow to harden; then break apart.
Yield: 12 servings

Chocolate has a very low melting point. It doesn't do well at excessively high heats (so be careful how long you bake your chocolate chip cookies). Always melt chocolate in a double boiler over very low heat, not letting the water boil.

WARMIN' UP HEARTS

Beverages Guaranteed to Chase Away the Winter Chill

The superiority of [hot] chocolate, both for health and nourishment, will soon give it the same preference over tea and coffee in America which it has in Spain.

THOMAS JEFFERSON (1743–1826),
third president of the United States

Best Eggnog

6 FRESH EGGS, BEATEN WELL

1 (14 OUNCE) CAN SWEETENED CONDENSED MILK

1 PINCH SALT

1 TEASPOON VANILLA EXTRACT

1 QUART MILK

⅔ CUP HEAVY WHIPPING CREAM

In a large mixing bowl, use a mixer to beat the eggs until thick and smooth. Blend in the condensed milk, salt, and vanilla; slowly add the milk. In a small bowl, beat the whipping cream until peaks start to form; then use a spatula to fold it into the egg mixture. Chill in the refrigerator and serve chilled. Servings may be sprinkled with nutmeg. Note: Please make your guests aware of the use of raw eggs.
Yield: 12 servings

Christmas Morning Coffee

1 POT (10 CUPS) BREWED COFFEE

⅓ CUP WATER

½ CUP SUGAR

¼ CUP UNSWEETENED COCOA

¼ TEASPOON GROUND CINNAMON

1 PINCH GRATED NUTMEG

SWEETENED WHIPPED TOPPING (OPTIONAL)

Prepare coffee. While coffee is brewing, heat water to a low boil in a large saucepan. Stir in sugar, cocoa, cinnamon, and nutmeg. Bring back to a low boil for 1 minute, stirring occasionally. Combine coffee with cocoa/spice mixture in saucepan. To serve, pour into mugs and top with sweetened whipped topping if desired.
Yield: 10 servings

Christmas Tea Mix

1 CUP INSTANT TEA MIX

2 CUPS POWDERED ORANGE DRINK MIX

3 CUPS SUGAR

½ CUP RED CINNAMON CANDIES

½ TEASPOON GROUND CLOVES

1 ENVELOPE LEMONADE MIX

Mix ingredients and store in an airtight container. To prepare one serving, add 1 heaping teaspoon to 1 cup hot water.
Yield: 7 cups of tea mix

Discover some old-fashioned holiday fun. Join a caroling group and visit local nursing homes and hospitals. Or just travel around the neighborhood spreading Christmas cheer. You'll brighten hearts as well as lift spirits (even if you do sing a little off-key!).

Creamy Orange Drink

6 CUPS ORANGE JUICE, DIVIDED

1 TEASPOON VANILLA EXTRACT

1 (3.4 OUNCE) PACKAGE INSTANT VANILLA PUDDING

1 ENVELOPE WHIPPED TOPPING MIX

In a large mixing bowl, combine half of orange juice with vanilla, pudding mix, and whipped topping mix. Beat until smooth; then mix in remaining juice. Chill thoroughly.
Yield: 6 to 8 servings

Festive Holiday Punch

8 CUPS APPLE JUICE

8 CUPS CRANBERRY JUICE COCKTAIL

2 RED APPLES, SLICED

2 CUPS CRANBERRIES

3 LITERS LEMON-LIME SODA

ICE CUBES AS NEEDED

Combine apple and cranberry juices in a punch bowl. Fifteen minutes before serving, add apple slices, cranberries, soda, and ice cubes. Do not stir. Yield: 24 servings

When you want ice in your punch bowl without a lot of extra water, try freezing all or part of your punch ingredients into ice cubes or one large chunk. For this punch, I like to combine the two juices with some cranberries and freeze it in a well-rounded bowl. The ice floats in the center of the punch bowl like an island that melts slowly. No worry about this ice cube getting into individual glasses.

Fireside Mocha Mix

2 CUPS NONDAIRY COFFEE CREAMER

1½ CUPS INSTANT COFFEE MIX

1½ CUPS HOT COCOA MIX

1½ CUPS SUGAR

1 TEASPOON GROUND CINNAMON

¼ TEASPOON GROUND NUTMEG

In a large bowl, combine all ingredients. Store mixture in an airtight container. To prepare one serving, stir 2 heaping tablespoons of mix into 1 cup boiling water.
Yield: 40 prepared cups

For a wonderful addition to a hot chocolate drink, try cinnamon sticks. Even better, dip your cinnamon sticks in melted chocolate and let them dry before using them to stir your drink. Then wrap up a few to go with a gift of drink mix.

Green Christmas Punch

2 ENVELOPES LEMON-LIME DRINK MIX

1½ CUPS SUGAR

2 QUARTS WATER

1 (20 OUNCE) CAN PINEAPPLE JUICE

1 (2 LITER) BOTTLE GINGER ALE

½ GALLON LIME SHERBET

MARASCHINO CHERRIES (OPTIONAL)

Dissolve drink mix and sugar in water. Stir in pineapple juice. Chill. To serve, blend lemon-lime mixture with ginger ale in a punch bowl. Scoop lime sherbet into punch bowl. If desired, place a maraschino cherry on each scoop of sherbet.
Yield: 25 to 30 servings

Holiday Punch

1 (3 OUNCE) PACKAGE CHERRY GELATIN

1 CUP BOILING WATER

1 (6 OUNCE) CAN FROZEN LEMONADE CONCENTRATE

3 CUPS COLD WATER

1 QUART CRANBERRY JUICE

ICE CUBES

1 (12 OUNCE) CAN GINGER ALE

Dissolve gelatin completely in boiling water. Stir in lemonade concentrate, cold water, and cranberry juice. Chill. Immediately before serving, pour mixture over ice cubes in a large punch bowl. Stir in ginger ale.
Yield: 25 to 30 servings

Hot Christmas Punch

1½ QUARTS WATER

2 CUPS SUGAR

JUICE OF 3 ORANGES

JUICE OF 1 LEMON

4 OUNCES RED CINNAMON CANDIES

1 (20 OUNCE) CAN PINEAPPLE JUICE

2 QUARTS CRANBERRY JUICE

In a large saucepan, boil water, sugar, orange juice, lemon juice, and cinnamon candies. Stir and boil until candies are dissolved. Add in pineapple juice and cranberry juice and cook over medium heat, stirring until punch is thoroughly heated. Serve hot.
Yield: 4 quarts

"Hot Vanilla"

4 CUPS MILK

4 TEASPOONS HONEY

½ TEASPOON VANILLA EXTRACT

GROUND CINNAMON

In a saucepan, heat milk until very hot. (Do not boil.) Remove from heat and stir in honey and vanilla. Divide between four mugs and sprinkle with cinnamon.
Yield: 4 servings

New Year's Eve Punch

1 (16 OUNCE) CAN FRUIT COCKTAIL

2 (6 OUNCE) CANS FROZEN ORANGE JUICE CONCENTRATE

2 (6 OUNCE) CANS FROZEN LEMONADE CONCENTRATE

2 (6 OUNCE) CANS FROZEN LIMEADE CONCENTRATE

2 (6 OUNCE) CANS FROZEN PINEAPPLE CONCENTRATE

1 PINT RASPBERRY SHERBET

Pour fruit cocktail into ring mold and freeze overnight.
Prepare frozen juices according to directions. Pour juices into a 10-quart punch bowl and mix well. When ready to serve, float fruit cocktail ring in punch. Scoop sherbet into the center of the fruit cocktail ring.
Yield: 18 to 24 servings

Dear heavenly Father, I admit I'm feeling a little less than cheerful this Christmas. I have so much I need to accomplish that I'm losing my passion and excitement for the holiday celebrations. Please help me keep my focus on only the things that matter—and to forget about the things that aren't important. Restore the joy of Christmas to my heart. Thank You, Lord. Amen.

Come to Bethlehem and see Christ whose birth the angels sing;
Come adore on bended knee, Christ the Lord, the newborn King.
Gloria, in excelsis Deo!
Gloria, in excelsis Deo!
TRADITIONAL FRENCH CAROL

Orange Eggnog Punch

1 QUART EGGNOG

1 (12 OUNCE) CAN FROZEN ORANGE JUICE CONCENTRATE, THAWED

1 (12 OUNCE) CAN GINGER ALE, CHILLED

In a pitcher, mix eggnog and orange juice concentrate until well blended.
Gradually pour in ginger ale and stir gently.
Yield: 8 servings

Orange Tea

7 CUPS WATER

1 (12 OUNCE) CAN FROZEN ORANGE JUICE CONCENTRATE

½ CUP SUGAR

2 TABLESPOONS LEMON JUICE

5 TEASPOONS INSTANT TEA MIX

1 TEASPOON WHOLE CLOVES

In a large saucepan, combine water, orange juice concentrate, sugar, lemon juice, and tea mix. Place cloves in tea ball or cheesecloth bag and add to saucepan. Simmer for 15 to 20 minutes. Remove cloves and serve hot. Yield: 8 servings

For the tea lover on your gift list, collect a variety of tea bags or loose tea, a tea ball strainer, a teacup, shortbread cookies, butter crackers, honey, and jam to fill a large teapot. Or place teapot and all in a basket lined with a tea towel.

Peppermint Christmas Punch

1 QUART EGGNOG

½ (2 LITER) BOTTLE CLUB SODA

½ GALLON VANILLA ICE CREAM, SOFTENED

PEPPERMINT CANDIES, CRUSHED

Stir together eggnog, club soda, and ice cream. Blend well. Sprinkle with crushed candies.
Yield: 8 to 10 servings

Pumpkin Nog

1 SMALL CAN PUMPKIN PUREE

1 PINT VANILLA ICE CREAM, SOFTENED

4 CUPS MILK

1 TEASPOON GROUND CINNAMON

½ TEASPOON GROUND NUTMEG

¼ TEASPOON GROUND GINGER

1 CUP WHIPPED TOPPING

Load a blender with small portions of pumpkin, ice cream, milk, and spices; blend thoroughly. Combine blended ingredients in a large pitcher and pour into mugs. Top with whipped cream and a sprinkle of cinnamon if desired. Yield: 10 servings

Snowy Cinnamon Cocoa

4 CUPS MILK

1 CUP CHOCOLATE SYRUP

1 TEASPOON GROUND CINNAMON

WHIPPED TOPPING

¼ CUP SEMISWEET CHOCOLATE CHIPS

Place milk and chocolate syrup in a microwave-safe bowl and stir. Cook on high for 3 to 4 minutes or until hot. Stir in cinnamon. Pour into four large mugs and garnish with whipped topping and chocolate chips.
Yield: 4 servings

Pick one night a week during Advent to sit down with your family and read through a short devotional and then pray together. Hot cocoa afterward is a must!

Sing to the LORD, praise his name;
proclaim his salvation day after day.

PSALM 96:2

Spicy Orange-Apple Punch

1½ QUARTS ORANGE JUICE

1 QUART APPLE JUICE

⅓ CUP LIGHT CORN SYRUP

24 WHOLE CLOVES

6 CINNAMON STICKS

12 THIN LEMON SLICES

Combine orange and apple juices, corn syrup, cloves, and cinnamon sticks
in a large saucepan. Gradually bring to a boil. Reduce heat and simmer at
least 5 to 10 minutes to blend flavors. Strain out the cloves and cinnamon.
Serve hot with a lemon slice.
Yield: 12 servings

Wassail

1 GALLON APPLE CIDER

2 CUPS ORANGE JUICE

1 (6 OUNCE) CAN FROZEN LEMONADE CONCENTRATE

2 TEASPOONS GROUND CINNAMON

1 TEASPOON GROUND NUTMEG

1 TEASPOON GROUND CLOVES

1 ORANGE, CUT INTO SLICES

Mix all ingredients in a large pan and slowly bring to a boil. Simmer for 10 minutes. Float orange slices in hot wassail before serving.
Yield: 18 to 20 servings

Wassail does well in the Crock-Pot at parties. Keep on the lowest setting. Stud 1 or 2 oranges with whole cloves and float them in the wassail. Use a dipper to serve the wassail into cups.

White Chocolate Coffee

3 OUNCES WHITE CHOCOLATE, GRATED

2 CUPS WHOLE MILK

2 CUPS HOT BREWED COFFEE

WHIPPED TOPPING (OPTIONAL)

Place grated white chocolate and milk in a microwave-safe bowl and heat for 2 minutes; stir until mixture is smooth and chocolate is melted completely. Stir in coffee. Serve in large mugs and top with whipped topping if desired. Yield: 4 servings

World's Best Cocoa

¼ CUP COCOA

½ CUP SUGAR

⅓ CUP HOT WATER

⅛ TEASPOON SALT

4 CUPS MILK

¾ TEASPOON VANILLA EXTRACT

Mix cocoa, sugar, water, and salt in a saucepan. Over medium heat, stir constantly until mixture boils. Continue to stir and boil for 1 minute. Add milk and heat. (Do not boil.) Remove from heat and add vanilla; stir well. Pour into four mugs and serve immediately.
Yield: 4 servings

KEEPIN' IT TRADITIONAL

All-Time Family Favorites

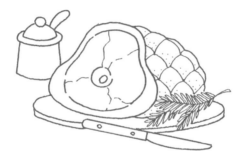

Strange to see how a good dinner and feasting reconciles everybody.

SAMUEL PEPYS (1633–1703), English naval administrator
and member of Parliament

Beef Burgundy

2 TABLESPOONS OLIVE OIL

1½ TO 2 POUNDS CUBED STEW MEAT

½ CUP CHOPPED ONION

1 (10 OUNCE) CAN CONDENSED CREAM OF MUSHROOM SOUP

¼ CUP RED WINE VINEGAR

¼ CUP REDUCED-SALT BEEF BROTH

¼ TEASPOON GARLIC POWDER

1 CUP SLICED FRESH MUSHROOMS

EGG NOODLES OR RICE, PREPARED

Heat oil in a skillet. Add stew meat and brown. Remove meat from heat. Add onions to pan and sauté until tender. In ovenproof casserole, mix meat, onion, soup, vinegar, broth, and garlic powder. Bake, covered, at 325° for 3 hours. The last 20 minutes, add mushrooms and return casserole to oven. Serve over egg noodles or rice.
Yield: 4 to 6 servings

Bierock Casserole

2 POUNDS LEAN GROUND BEEF

1 MEDIUM ONION, DICED

1 SMALL HEAD CABBAGE, CHOPPED

SALT AND PEPPER TO TASTE

1 (36 COUNT) PACKAGE FROZEN ROLLS

In a large skillet, brown meat with diced onion. Add cabbage; cover and cook until cabbage is tender. Add salt and pepper to taste. Grease two 9 x 13-inch baking pans. Place 18 rolls in each pan. Let rise. Press down gently. Spoon cabbage mixture on top of rolls in one pan. Flip the rolls from the other pan over the top of the cabbage. Press down lightly. Bake at 350° for 30 to 35 minutes or until rolls are browned.
Yield: 9 servings

Lord, Thank You for one of the most precious gifts I've ever received—the gift of my family. I'm so glad they're a part of my life. Amen.

Give thanks to the LORD, for he is good.

PSALM 136:1

Broiled Shrimp

1 CUP BUTTER

2 GARLIC CLOVES, MINCED

¼ CUP LEMON JUICE

½ TEASPOON SALT

¼ TEASPOON FRESHLY GROUND BLACK PEPPER

2 POUNDS LARGE SHRIMP, PEELED AND DEVEINED

CHOPPED FRESH PARSLEY

In a saucepan over low heat, melt butter with garlic, but don't allow garlic to scorch. Remove from heat and add lemon juice, salt, and pepper. Place shrimp in a shallow baking dish and pour sauce over shrimp. Broil the shrimp 4 to 5 inches from the heating element for 6 to 8 minutes. Turn and baste the shrimp halfway through. When done, shrimp should be pink and tender. Garnish with chopped fresh parsley.
Yield: 6 servings

Chicken Diane

4 LARGE BONELESS CHICKEN BREAST HALVES

½ TEASPOON SALT

½ TEASPOON BLACK PEPPER

2 TABLESPOONS OLIVE OIL, DIVIDED

2 TABLESPOONS BUTTER OR MARGARINE, DIVIDED

3 TABLESPOONS CHOPPED FRESH CHIVES

JUICE OF ½ LEMON

3 TABLESPOONS CHOPPED FRESH PARSLEY

2 TEASPOONS DIJON MUSTARD

¼ CUP CHICKEN BROTH

Place each chicken breast between two sheets of waxed paper and pound to flatten slightly. Sprinkle chicken with salt and pepper. Set aside. In a large skillet, heat 1 tablespoon each of oil and butter. Cook each chicken breast in skillet for 4 minutes on each side. Transfer to a warm serving platter. Add chives, lemon juice, parsley, and mustard to skillet. Cook for 15 seconds, whisking constantly. Whisk in the broth and stir until sauce is smooth. Whisk in remaining oil and butter. Pour sauce over chicken and serve immediately.
Yield: 4 servings

Chicken Divan Casserole

4 BONELESS, SKINLESS CHICKEN
BREASTS

1 FRESH ROSEMARY SPRIG

1 TEASPOON SALT, DIVIDED

1/4 TEASPOON BLACK PEPPER

2 TABLESPOONS BUTTER OR
MARGARINE

1/4 CUP ALL-PURPOSE FLOUR

1 CUP MILK

1 EGG YOLK, BEATEN

1 (8 OUNCE) CARTON SOUR CREAM

1/2 CUP MAYONNAISE

1/2 TEASPOON GRATED LEMON
PEEL

2 TABLESPOONS LEMON JUICE

1/4 TEASPOON CURRY POWDER

2 (10 OUNCE) PACKAGES FROZEN
BROCCOLI SPEARS, THAWED
AND DRAINED

1/3 CUP GRATED PARMESAN CHEESE

PAPRIKA

Place chicken breasts, rosemary, 1/2 teaspoon salt, and pepper in a large saucepan; add water to cover. Bring water to a boil. Cover, reduce heat, and simmer for 10 to 15 minutes or until chicken is tender. Drain, reserving 1/2 cup broth. Discard rosemary sprig. Cool chicken slightly, then cut into bite-sized pieces; set chicken aside.

Melt butter in a heavy saucepan over low heat; add flour, stirring until smooth. Cook for 1 minute, stirring constantly. Gradually add milk and reserved broth; cook over medium heat, stirring constantly, until thickened and bubbly. Stir small amount of hot mixture into egg yolk; add back into remaining hot mixture, stirring constantly. Cook for 1 minute. Remove from heat; stir in sour cream, mayonnaise, lemon rind, lemon juice, 1/2 teaspoon salt, and curry powder. Layer half each of broccoli, chicken, and sauce in a greased 2-quart casserole. Repeat layers. Sprinkle with grated Parmesan cheese and paprika. Bake, uncovered, at 350° for 30 to 35 minutes.

Yield: 4 to 6 servings

Cornish Hens with Basil-Walnut Sauce

1 BUNCH FRESH BASIL

½ CUP GRATED PARMESAN CHEESE

1 GARLIC CLOVE

SALT AND PEPPER TO TASTE

¼ CUP WALNUTS

2 CORNISH GAME HENS, SPLIT
   AND QUARTERED

BUTTER

½ CUP CHICKEN STOCK

½ CUP HEAVY CREAM

ADDITIONAL BASIL AND WALNUTS
FOR GARNISH (OPTIONAL)

In food processor basket, combine first five ingredients. Puree to a smooth paste. Set aside. In a large skillet, cook the hens in butter until tender. Transfer to a warm platter. Drain the grease from the skillet and pour in chicken stock. Cook until stock is reduced by half. Add the cream, and again reduce to half. Stir in 2 tablespoons of the basil-walnut paste. Add additional salt and pepper if needed. Pour sauce over the hens, and garnish with basil and walnuts.

Yield: 4 servings

Create a centerpiece that grows. Gather cotton quilt batting (avoid polyester), a large dinner plate, a tall fat candle, ¼ cup sproutable chive or lentil seed (available at a health food store), plastic wrap, and a spray bottle full of water. Cover all but the center and outer edge of the plate with a layer of batting. Spray water over the batting. Scatter the seeds on top, and spray with more water. Carefully tip the plate to pour off any extra water. Tightly cover the plate with plastic wrap and put it in a well-lit place, but not in direct sunlight. Spray the batting every two days. When you see the first sprouts, remove the plastic wrap, then spray with water daily. In 10 to 14 days, you should have a wreath of green sprouts. Place a candle in the center. The centerpiece will need to be kept in a sunlit place and watered regularly.

Glazed Ham

1 (2 LITER) BOTTLE DR PEPPER

1 TABLESPOON GROUND CLOVES

1 TEASPOON GROUND CINNAMON

1 (7 TO 10 POUND) FULLY COOKED HAM

WHOLE CLOVES

Place ham in a roasting pan and cover with a mixture of Dr Pepper and spices. Bake ham at 325° for 1½ hours. Remove from oven and score top of ham. Stud ham with cloves.

MIX TOGETHER:

1 TEASPOON GROUND CINNAMON

1 TEASPOON DRY MUSTARD

DR PEPPER

Add enough Dr Pepper to form a paste. Brush mixture over scored ham.

MIX TOGETHER:

1 CUP BROWN SUGAR

¼ CUP DR PEPPER, OR ENOUGH TO FORM A PASTE

Brush final mixture over ham. Bake an additional 1½ hours or until ham reaches an internal temperature of 140°.
Yield: 12 to 14 servings

Ham with Apple Relish

1 TEASPOON GROUND CLOVES

1 (3 TO 4 POUND) FULLY COOKED BONELESS HAM

4 MEDIUM TART APPLES, PEELED AND CHOPPED

2 CUPS SUGAR

1 CUP CHOPPED DRIED APRICOTS

½ CUP DRIED CRANBERRIES

½ CUP GOLDEN RAISINS

¼ CUP WHITE VINEGAR

2 TABLESPOONS GRATED ORANGE PEEL

½ TEASPOON GROUND GINGER

Rub cloves over ham. Wrap ham tightly in foil and bake at 325° for 1 to 1½ hours or until internal temperature reaches 140°. Meanwhile, combine remaining ingredients in a saucepan for the relish. Stirring constantly, bring mixture to a boil. Reduce heat and simmer for 25 to 30 minutes or until thickened. Serve relish over ham slices.
Yield: 8 to 10 servings

Spend some quality time with your family this Christmas. Cook up a special dinner of family favorites and enjoy dessert while watching a great Christmas classic on TV.

Home-Style Roast Beef

1 (10 TO 12 POUND) BOTTOM ROUND BEEF ROAST

1 (14½ OUNCE) CAN CHICKEN BROTH

1 (10¼ OUNCE) CAN BEEF GRAVY

1 (10¾ OUNCE) CAN CONDENSED CREAM OF CELERY SOUP

¼ CUP WATER

¼ CUP WORCESTERSHIRE SAUCE

¼ CUP SOY SAUCE

3 TABLESPOONS DRIED PARSLEY FLAKES

3 TABLESPOONS DILL WEED

2 TABLESPOONS DRIED THYME

4½ TEASPOONS GARLIC POWDER

1 TEASPOON CELERY SALT

1 TEASPOON BLACK PEPPER

1 LARGE ONION, SLICED INTO RINGS

Place roast in a large roasting pan, fat side up. Prick meat with meat fork. In a bowl, combine broth, gravy, soup, water, Worcestershire, and soy sauce. Pour mixture evenly over the roast, then sprinkle with seasonings. Place onion rings over the roast. Bake, uncovered, at 325° for 2½ to 3½ hours or until meat reaches desired doneness. Meat thermometer should read 140° for a rare roast, 160° for a medium roast, and 170° for a well-done roast. Let stand for 15 to 20 minutes before slicing.
Yield: 25 to 30 servings

Hot Turkey Salad

3 CUPS DICED COOKED TURKEY

4 HARD-BOILED EGGS, CHOPPED

2 CUPS DICED CELERY

1 CUP SLICED FRESH MUSHROOMS

2 TABLESPOONS DICED ONION

¾ CUP MAYONNAISE

1 TABLESPOON LEMON JUICE

½ CUP CORNFLAKE CRUMBS

2 TABLESPOONS BUTTER OR MARGARINE, MELTED

In a large bowl, combine turkey, eggs, celery, mushrooms, onion, mayonnaise, and lemon juice. Transfer to a 9 x 13-inch baking dish. Top with cornflake crumbs and drizzle with melted butter. Bake at 350° for 30 minutes.
Yield: 6 to 8 servings

Italian Turkey

1½ POUNDS GROUND SALT PORK

1 GARLIC CLOVE, MINCED

3 TEASPOONS GROUND SAGE

2½ TO 3⅓ TEASPOONS CHILI POWDER

SALT AND PEPPER TO TASTE

1 (10 TO 12 POUND) TURKEY

Combine first five ingredients and spread over turkey. Bake at 350° for 4½ hours or until done. Remove pork mixture from turkey and place in a large bowl; crumble mixture with a fork. Debone turkey and chop meat into small pieces. Blend turkey with pork mixture. Serve as loose meat or with rolls for sandwiches.

Yield: 25 to 30 servings

Jackie's Ham Balls

2½ POUNDS HAM LOAF MIX*

1 CUP GRAHAM CRACKER CRUMBS

¼ TEASPOON BLACK PEPPER

2 EGGS, BEATEN

1 CUP MILK

⅓ CUP WHITE VINEGAR

1½ CUPS BROWN SUGAR

1 CUP WATER

1 TEASPOON DRY MUSTARD

Combine meat, graham cracker crumbs, pepper, eggs, and milk. Form into balls, approximately 5 to 6 per pound. In a saucepan combine vinegar, brown sugar, water, and mustard for the glaze and bring to a boil. Pour glaze over ham balls and bake at 350° for about 1 hour.
Yield: 12 to 15 ham balls

*You can get ham loaf mix at the meat market. It's just ground ham with fresh pork.

Lemon-Herb Turkey Breast

1 (8 TO 9 POUND) BONE-IN TURKEY BREAST

3 TABLESPOONS FRESH LEMON JUICE, DIVIDED

2 TABLESPOONS OLIVE OIL, DIVIDED

2 GARLIC CLOVES, CRUSHED

1¼ TEASPOONS SALT

1 TEASPOON GRATED LEMON PEEL

1 TEASPOON DRIED THYME

1 TEASPOON FRESHLY GROUND BLACK PEPPER

½ TEASPOON GROUND SAGE

LEMON-PEPPER SEASONING TO TASTE

Rinse turkey in cold water and pat dry. Loosen skin from turkey with fingers, but leave skin attached to meat. In a small bowl, combine 1 tablespoon lemon juice, 1 tablespoon oil, garlic, salt, lemon peel, thyme, pepper, and sage. Spread evenly under turkey skin. Combine remaining lemon juice and oil; set aside. Place turkey on a rack in a shallow roasting pan sprayed with cooking spray. Bake, uncovered, at 350° for 2½ to 3 hours or until meat thermometer reads 170°, basting every 15 to 20 minutes with lemon juice and oil mixture. Let stand for 10 to 15 minutes before carving. Yield: 16 servings

Mediterranean Chicken

½ CUP FETA CHEESE

¼ CUP MINCED GREEN ONIONS

BLACK PEPPER TO TASTE

4 BONELESS CHICKEN BREASTS

3 TABLESPOONS BUTTER

2 SMALL SHALLOTS, MINCED

¼ TEASPOON MINCED FRESH BASIL

3 SMALL GARLIC CLOVES, MINCED

1 TEASPOON DRIED OREGANO

1 CUP SLICED FRESH MUSHROOMS

1 TABLESPOON FLOUR

¾ CUP CHICKEN STOCK

½ CUP DICED TOMATOES

1 TABLESPOON FETA CHEESE

In a small bowl, combine ½ cup feta cheese, green onions, and pepper. Place chicken breasts between sheets of waxed paper and pound to flatten slightly. Divide the cheese filling equally between the chicken breasts. Fold the chicken around the filling, and place each breast in a shallow baking dish. Bake at 350° for 35 to 40 minutes.

Meanwhile, melt the butter in a small skillet. Add the shallots, basil, garlic, oregano, and mushrooms. Sauté briefly. Add flour and stir until blended. Slowly pour in half of the chicken stock. Stir constantly until sauce is smooth and begins to thicken. Add remaining chicken stock; then stir in tomatoes and 1 tablespoon feta cheese. Simmer for 10 minutes. Serve sauce over baked chicken breasts.

Yield: 4 servings

Orange Duck

½ CUP ORANGE JUICE

½ CUP APPLE JELLY

1 DASH PEPPER

1 (5 POUND) DRESSED DUCK

SALT AND PEPPER TO TASTE

1 LARGE STALK CELERY, CUT INTO 2-INCH PIECES

1 SMALL ONION, QUARTERED

⅔ CUP LONG-GRAIN RICE, UNCOOKED

1 (12¾ OUNCE) PACKAGE INSTANT WILD RICE

⅓ CUP CHOPPED FRESH PARSLEY

Combine orange juice, jelly, and pepper in a small saucepan. Cook over medium heat until jelly melts and mixture bubbles, stirring frequently. Remove from heat and keep warm.

Rub cavity of duck with salt and pepper; place celery and onion pieces in cavity. Place duck, breast side up, on a rack in a roasting pan. Baste lightly with melted jelly mixture. Bake, uncovered, at 375° for 1 hour, basting frequently with jelly mixture. If duck starts to brown too much, cover loosely with aluminum foil. Bake for an additional 1 to 1½ hours or until meat thermometer registers 185° when placed in thickest part of duck breast, basting frequently. Prepare long-grain rice and wild rice according to package directions. Combine cooked rice and parsley; stir well. Spoon onto a serving platter. Place duck on top of rice.
Yield: 4 servings

Oven-Fried Chicken

¼ CUP BUTTER OR MARGARINE, MELTED AND DIVIDED

⅓ CUP CORNMEAL

⅓ CUP FLOUR

¼ TEASPOON PAPRIKA

¼ TEASPOON SALT

¼ TEASPOON GARLIC POWDER

2 TABLESPOONS GRATED PARMESAN CHEESE

4 TO 6 BONELESS, SKINLESS CHICKEN BREASTS

Pour half of butter in a long baking dish and set aside. Combine the next six ingredients in a sealed plastic bag. Shake each piece of chicken in mixture to coat. Place chicken pieces in baking dish, and pour remaining butter over the chicken. Bake at 350° for 1 hour and 15 minutes.
Yield: 4 to 6 servings

Create a festive atmosphere in your dining room by hanging stockings on all the chairs. A week before Christmas, begin leaving small gifts or heartfelt notes in the stockings. Your family will be reminded of how special they are to you.

Let us love one another, for love comes from God.

1 JOHN 4:7

Porcupine Meatballs

1 CAN CONDENSED TOMATO SOUP

1 POUND GROUND BEEF

½ CUP UNCOOKED WHITE RICE

½ CUP WATER

1 TEASPOON SALT

½ TEASPOON BLACK PEPPER

1 SMALL ONION, MINCED

½ TABLESPOON DRIED PARSLEY FLAKES

1 TEASPOON WORCESTERSHIRE SAUCE

Mix tomato soup with one soup can of water. Set aside. In a large mixing bowl, combine remaining ingredients. Form meat mixture into 1½-inch balls. Place meatballs in a greased casserole. Pour soup and water mixture over meatballs. Cover and bake at 350° for 45 minutes.
Yield: 4 servings

Reuben Casserole

8 SLICES RYE BREAD, CUBED AND DIVIDED

1 CUP SOUR CREAM

1 LARGE ONION, DICED

1 (16 OUNCE) CAN SAUERKRAUT, DRAINED

1 (12 OUNCE) CAN CORNED BEEF

12 TO 16 OUNCES GRATED SWISS CHEESE

½ CUP BUTTER OR MARGARINE, MELTED

Layer half of the bread cubes in a greased 9 x 13-inch casserole. Blend sour cream and onion; spread over bread. Spread sauerkraut on top. Crumble corned beef over sauerkraut. Add shredded cheese, then top with remaining bread; drizzle with melted butter. Bake at 350° for 45 minutes.
Yield: 6 to 8 servings

Roasted Leg of Lamb

1½ TABLESPOONS FRESH ROSEMARY LEAVES

½ CUP FRESH MINT LEAVES

4 GARLIC CLOVES, CRUSHED

½ CUP RASPBERRY VINEGAR

¼ CUP SOY SAUCE

½ CUP BEEF STOCK

3 TABLESPOONS CRUSHED PEPPERCORN, DIVIDED

1 (5 TO 6 POUND) LEG OF LAMB

2 TABLESPOONS DIJON MUSTARD

In a shallow dish, combine rosemary leaves, mint leaves, garlic, vinegar, soy sauce, beef stock, and 1 tablespoon crushed peppercorn. Place lamb in mixture and marinate for 8 to 9 hours, turning occasionally.

Remove lamb from dish and drain, reserving marinade. Roll the roast and tie with string. Spread mustard over lamb and sprinkle with remaining peppercorn. Bake at 350° for 1½ hours. Bake for an additional 15 minutes for well-done meat. Let roast stand for 15 minutes before serving.
Yield: 6 to 8 servings

Rotisserie-Style Chicken

1 (4 TO 5 POUND) WHOLE CHICKEN

2 TEASPOONS SALT

1 TEASPOON PAPRIKA

½ TEASPOON ONION POWDER

½ TEASPOON GROUND THYME

½ TEASPOON BLACK PEPPER

½ TEASPOON DRIED OREGANO

¼ TEASPOON CAYENNE PEPPER

¼ TEASPOON GARLIC POWDER

1 ONION, QUARTERED

Remove giblets from chicken. Rinse out chicken cavity and pat chicken dry. Set aside. In a small bowl, mix together spices. Rub spice mixture on the inside and outside of chicken. Place onion inside chicken cavity. Place chicken in a sealable bag and refrigerate overnight.

Remove chicken from bag and place it in a roasting pan. Bake, uncovered, at 250° for 5 hours or until internal temperature reaches 180°. Yield: 4 servings

Nifty napkin rings for your family dinner start with a hodgepodge of old spoons and forks from family collections or flea markets. Use your hands to bend the pliable ones around a paper towel tube. Let the ends meet side-by-side, and you have a delightful napkin ring. Make an extra set for a gift.

Raspberry Chicken

4 BONELESS, SKINLESS CHICKEN BREASTS

2 TABLESPOONS BUTTER

¼ CUP FINELY CHOPPED ONION

¼ CUP RASPBERRY VINEGAR

¼ CUP CHICKEN BROTH

¼ CUP HEAVY CREAM

1 TABLESPOON CANNED CRUSHED TOMATOES

¼ CUP FROZEN RASPBERRIES

Between sheets of waxed paper, pound chicken to flatten slightly. In a large skillet, melt butter. Cook each chicken breast for 3 minutes on each side. Transfer from skillet to a warmed platter. Add onion to skillet and sauté until onions are translucent. Add vinegar and cook until syrup is reduced to approximately 1 tablespoon. Whisk in the chicken broth, cream, and tomatoes. Simmer for 1 minute. Return chicken breasts to skillet and simmer gently in the sauce, basting frequently, until chicken is done, about 5 minutes. Remove the chicken and add raspberries to the skillet. Cook over low heat for 1 minute. Pour the sauce over the chicken and serve immediately.
Yield: 4 servings

A fun and simple idea for your Christmas dinner get-together: Tie a small ornament with ribbon around the napkins at place settings. Your guests will appreciate these thoughtful little gifts.

Every good and perfect gift is from above.

JAMES 1:17

Roast Turkey and Corn Bread Dressing

1 (12 TO 14 POUND) WHOLE TURKEY

CORN BREAD DRESSING (RECIPE ON PAGE 82)

½ CUP BUTTER OR MARGARINE, MELTED

SALT AND PEPPER TO TASTE

Remove giblets and neck from turkey. Rinse turkey thoroughly inside and out; pat dry. Lightly pack corn bread dressing into body cavity of turkey. Tuck the drumsticks under the folds of skin or tie together with string. Place turkey on a rack in a roasting pan, breast side up; brush entire surface of bird with melted butter. Sprinkle with salt and pepper. Insert meat thermometer into meaty part of thigh, making sure it does not touch bone. Bake turkey at 325° for 4½ to 5½ hours or until meat thermometer reads 185° and stuffing has reached at least 165°. Baste turkey occasionally with melted butter. Tent foil over turkey if it begins to brown too quickly. Let turkey stand 15 to 20 minutes before carving.
Yield: 20 servings

Corn Bread Dressing

4 STALKS CELERY, DICED

2 MEDIUM ONIONS, DICED

¼ CUP BUTTER OR MARGARINE, MELTED

6 CUPS PREPARED CRUMBLED CORN BREAD

5 SLICES DAY-OLD BREAD, WHEAT OR WHITE, CRUMBLED

1 POUND BULK PORK SAUSAGE, COOKED AND DRAINED

1½ CUPS FINELY CHOPPED COOKED HAM

¾ CUP ALMONDS, TOASTED AND CHOPPED

¾ CUP CHOPPED FRESH PARSLEY

1½ TEASPOONS BLACK PEPPER

1 TEASPOON POULTRY SEASONING

1 TEASPOON GROUND SAGE

2 CUPS CHICKEN BROTH

1 EGG, LIGHTLY BEATEN

Sauté celery and onion in butter until tender. Combine with breads, sausage, ham, almonds, and seasonings in a large bowl; toss well. Add broth and egg to corn bread mixture; stir well.

If desired, dressing may be baked separately from turkey in a lightly greased 9 x 13-inch baking dish. Bake, uncovered, at 350° for 45 minutes to 1 hour or until lightly browned. Unstuffed turkey should be baked 5 minutes less per pound than stuffed turkey.

Seafood Bake

1 CUP CHOPPED ONION

1 CUP CHOPPED CELERY

4 TABLESPOONS BUTTER

½ POUND CRABMEAT AND/OR LOBSTER MEAT

¼ POUND MEDIUM SHRIMP

¼ POUND SCALLOPS

½ TEASPOON GARLIC POWDER

½ TEASPOON SALT

½ TEASPOON BLACK PEPPER

¼ CUP FLOUR

2 CUPS MILK

2 CUPS SHREDDED MILD CHEDDAR CHEESE

1 TO 2 CUPS BUTTERED BREAD CRUMBS OR CRACKER CRUMBS (OPTIONAL)

In a large skillet, sauté onions and celery in butter until they start to soften; add crabmeat, shrimp, and scallops, tossing in the butter. Season with garlic powder, salt, and pepper. Sprinkle meat with flour, allowing butter to absorb. Slowly add milk, stirring constantly over low heat until well blended and some thickening is apparent. Mix in cheese, then place in a greased casserole. Bake, uncovered, at 350° for 25 to 30 minutes.
Yield: 4 servings

Shrimp with Pasta

16 OUNCES VERMICELLI

SALT AND PEPPER TO TASTE

½ CUP BUTTER

½ CUP OLIVE OIL

4 GARLIC CLOVES, MINCED

24 LARGE SHRIMP, PEELED AND DEVEINED

8 LARGE FRESH MUSHROOMS, SLICED

1 CUP CHOPPED FRESH PARSLEY

ROMANO CHEESE

Cook vermicelli in boiling water for 10 minutes. Drain and rinse in cold water. Toss noodles with salt and pepper and set aside. In a large skillet, heat butter and oil. Add garlic, shrimp, and mushrooms. Cook until shrimp turns pink, about 5 minutes. Toss in vermicelli and heat through. Transfer to a warmed platter and sprinkle with parsley and cheese.
Yield: 4 servings

Spicy Honey-Citrus Cornish Hens

4 CORNISH GAME HENS

1 ORANGE, UNPEELED AND QUARTERED

1 LEMON, UNPEELED AND QUARTERED

¼ CUP APRICOT PRESERVES

¼ CUP HONEY

1 TABLESPOON GRATED ORANGE PEEL

1 TABLESPOON GRATED LEMON PEEL

1 TABLESPOON LEMON JUICE

1 TABLESPOON DIJON MUSTARD

1 TEASPOON GROUND GINGER

½ TEASPOON CAYENNE PEPPER

SALT AND FRESHLY GROUND PEPPER TO TASTE

Remove giblets from hens. Rinse and pat dry. Place one orange wedge and one lemon wedge in each hen and place in a roasting pan. Combine the remaining ingredients in a small saucepan and simmer for 5 minutes. Brush hens with mixture and bake at 350° for approximately 1¼ hours, until hens are tender. While baking, brush hens occasionally with sauce.
Yield: 4 servings

Sweet-and-Sour Chops

4 LOIN-CUT PORK CHOPS, EXCESS FAT TRIMMED

4 MEDIUM POTATOES, CUT INTO ¾-INCH SLICES

2 (10 OUNCE) CANS CONDENSED CREAM OF MUSHROOM SOUP

1 SMALL ONION, DICED

1 GARLIC CLOVE, MINCED

3 TABLESPOONS HONEY

3 TABLESPOONS PREPARED MUSTARD

3 TABLESPOONS LEMON JUICE

½ TEASPOON WORCESTERSHIRE SAUCE

½ TEASPOON DRIED PARSLEY FLAKES

½ TEASPOON GROUND SAGE

½ TEASPOON GROUND THYME

SALT AND PEPPER TO TASTE

In a large skillet, quickly brown pork chops on both sides. Place pork chops in a large baking dish and set aside. Boil potatoes in salted water until slightly softened. Drain well and layer over pork chops. In a large bowl, combine remaining ingredients; stir until thoroughly combined. Pour mixture over potatoes and chops. Bake at 350° for 25 to 30 minutes or until pork chops are done.
Yield: 4 servings

Traditional Christmas Turkey

1 (10 TO 12 POUND) WHOLE TURKEY

6 TABLESPOONS BUTTER, CUT INTO SLICES

4 CUPS WARM WATER

3 CUBES CHICKEN BOUILLON

2 TABLESPOONS DRIED PARSLEY FLAKES

2 TABLESPOONS MINCED ONION

2 TABLESPOONS SEASONED SALT

2 TABLESPOONS POULTRY SEASONING

Rinse turkey. Remove neck and discard giblets. Place turkey in a roasting pan. Separate the skin over the breast and place slices of butter between the skin and breast meat. In a small bowl, dissolve bouillon in the water. Stir in parsley and minced onion and pour mixture over the top of the turkey. Sprinkle turkey with seasoned salt and poultry seasoning. Cover with foil and bake at 350° for 3½ to 4 hours, until internal temperature of turkey reaches 180°. Remove foil during the last 45 minutes to brown turkey. Yield: 12 servings

Have a Christmas "picnic" with your family. Even though it's blustery outside, you can still enjoy this summertime treat indoors. Spread a blanket on the living room floor, pack simple foods in a picnic basket (complete with holiday-themed napkins and dinnerware), and feast in front of a blazing fire. Top it off with marshmallows roasted over the fire.

Turkey Scaloppine

½ TO ¾ POUND TURKEY CUTLETS

½ CUP FLOUR

½ TEASPOON SALT

¼ TEASPOON BLACK PEPPER

¼ TEASPOON DRIED BASIL

3 TABLESPOONS BUTTER OR MARGARINE, DIVIDED

2 TABLESPOONS OLIVE OIL

1 GARLIC CLOVE, MINCED

¼ POUND SLICED FRESH MUSHROOMS

2 TABLESPOONS LEMON JUICE

⅓ CUP CHICKEN BROTH

¼ CUP WHITE WINE OR ADDITIONAL CHICKEN BROTH

Between sheets of waxed paper, pound cutlets to ⅛-inch thickness.
Combine flour, salt, pepper, and basil. Dredge cutlets in seasoned flour and
shake off excess. In a skillet, melt 2 tablespoons butter. Add oil and stir
in garlic. Brown each cutlet until golden, approximately 3 minutes. Place
browned meat in ovenproof casserole. Melt remaining tablespoon of butter
in skillet; add mushrooms. Sauté until mushrooms have softened; spoon
over meat. In the same skillet, combine lemon juice with broth and wine.
Cook until heated through. Pour over casserole. Bake at 325° for 30 to 35
minutes.
Yield: 4 servings

ADDIN' THE TRIMMINGS

Seasonal Sides and Salads

At all events, the perfect dinner necessarily includes the perfect salad.

GEORGE ELLWANGER (1816–1906), *Pleasures of the Table*

SIDES

Almond Rice

1¾ CUPS WATER

½ CUP ORANGE JUICE

½ TEASPOON SALT

1 CUP UNCOOKED LONG-GRAIN RICE

2 TABLESPOONS BUTTER OR MARGARINE

2 TABLESPOONS BROWN SUGAR

½ CUP SLICED NATURAL ALMONDS

1 TEASPOON MINCED CRYSTALLIZED GINGER

¼ TEASPOON GRATED ORANGE PEEL

ADDITIONAL ORANGE PEEL (OPTIONAL)

In a medium saucepan, bring water, orange juice, and salt to a boil;
gradually add rice, stirring constantly. Cover, reduce heat, and simmer for
20 to 25 minutes or until rice is tender and liquid is absorbed. Meanwhile,
melt butter and brown sugar in a small skillet over medium heat. Stir
in almonds and ginger; sauté for 2 minutes or until almonds are lightly
browned. Add almond mixture and grated orange peel to rice; stir gently to
combine. Garnish with additional orange peel if desired.
Yield: 4 servings

Artichoke Spinach Casserole

1 (8 OUNCE) CARTON SOUR CREAM

½ CUP MAYONNAISE

3 TABLESPOONS LEMON JUICE

½ TEASPOON GARLIC POWDER

¼ TEASPOON ONION POWDER

¼ TEASPOON SALT

¼ TEASPOON BLACK PEPPER

2 TABLESPOONS BUTTER OR MARGARINE

1 POUND SLICED FRESH MUSHROOMS

⅓ CUP CHICKEN BROTH

1 TABLESPOON FLOUR

½ CUP MILK

4 (10 OUNCE) PACKAGES FROZEN SPINACH, THAWED AND DRAINED

2 (14½ OUNCE) CANS DICED TOMATOES, DRAINED

2 (14 OUNCE) CANS ARTICHOKE HEARTS, DRAINED AND CHOPPED

In a small bowl, combine sour cream, mayonnaise, lemon juice, garlic powder, onion powder, salt, and pepper. Mix thoroughly; set aside. In a large skillet, heat butter until melted. Add mushrooms and sauté until they begin to soften. Pour in broth and cook until mushrooms are tender. Remove mushrooms from skillet and set aside. In a small bowl, whisk together flour and milk. Add to skillet and bring to a boil. Cook for 2 minutes, stirring constantly. Remove from heat and stir in spinach, tomatoes, and mushrooms. Layer half of the artichoke hearts in a 9 x 13-inch casserole. Layer half of the spinach mixture over artichokes. Spoon half of the sour cream mixture on top. Repeat layers. Bake, uncovered, at 350° for 30 to 35 minutes.
Yield: 12 servings

Artichokes au Gratin

2 (9 OUNCE) PACKAGES FROZEN
ARTICHOKE HEARTS

¼ CUP BUTTER OR MARGARINE

⅓ CUP FLOUR

¾ TEASPOON SALT

¼ TEASPOON BLACK PEPPER

1 TEASPOON ONION POWDER

¼ TEASPOON DRY MUSTARD

1½ CUPS MILK

1 EGG, LIGHTLY BEATEN

1 CUP SHREDDED MILD CHEDDAR
CHEESE, DIVIDED

¼ CUP DRY BREAD CRUMBS

PAPRIKA

Cook artichokes according to package directions. Drain and reserve ½ cup of cooking liquid. Melt butter in a saucepan over low heat; stir in flour, salt, pepper, onion powder, and dry mustard. Cook and stir until flour mixture is smooth and bubbly; gradually add reserved cooking liquid and milk. Cook over low heat, stirring constantly, until thickened. Remove from heat. Combine beaten egg with ½ cup shredded cheese. Gradually stir sauce mixture into egg and cheese mixture. Place artichokes in a greased baking dish in a single layer. Pour sauce over artichokes; sprinkle with remaining cheese, bread crumbs, and paprika. Bake at 425° for 20 to 25 minutes.
Yield: 6 servings

Counter space is often a precious commodity in a busy holiday kitchen. For a quick and handy extra countertop, set up your ironing board and cover it with a plastic tablecloth.

Blue Cheese Green Beans

2 OUNCES BLUE CHEESE,
CRUMBLED AND DIVIDED

3 TABLESPOONS HALF-AND-HALF

2 TABLESPOONS WHITE WINE
VINEGAR

1 TABLESPOON GRATED PARMESAN
CHEESE

½ TEASPOON DRIED OREGANO

¼ TEASPOON COARSELY GROUND
BLACK PEPPER

⅛ TEASPOON SUGAR

¼ CUP VEGETABLE OIL

1 POUND FRESH GREEN BEANS

¼ TEASPOON SALT

BLACK PEPPER TO TASTE

1 (2 OUNCE) JAR DICED PIMIENTO,
DRAINED

4 SLICES BACON, COOKED AND
CRUMBLED

In blender, combine 1 ounce blue cheese, half-and-half, vinegar, Parmesan cheese, oregano, pepper, and sugar. Cover and process until smooth. With blender running, add vegetable oil in a slow, steady stream. Process just until blended; set dressing mixture aside.

Wash beans; trim ends and remove strings. Cook beans in a small amount of boiling salted water for 15 to 20 minutes or until tender. Drain and arrange beans on a serving platter. Sprinkle with salt and pepper. Pour blue cheese dressing mixture over beans. Top with pimiento, 1 ounce crumbled blue cheese, and crumbled bacon.
Yield: 4 servings

Include the recipe for your "famous" dish with your Christmas cards this year. Print out several copies on Christmassy paper and add a personal note from you.

Christmas is the season for kindling the fire of hospitality in the hall, the genial flame of charity in the heart.
WASHINGTON IRVING

Cheesy Onion Casserole

2 TABLESPOONS BUTTER OR MARGARINE

3 LARGE SWEET ONIONS, SLICED INTO RINGS

2 CUPS SHREDDED SWISS CHEESE, DIVIDED

BLACK PEPPER TO TASTE

1 (10¾ OUNCE) CONDENSED CREAM OF CHICKEN SOUP

⅔ CUP MILK

1 TEASPOON SOY SAUCE

8 SLICES FRENCH BREAD, BUTTERED ON BOTH SIDES

Melt butter in a large skillet. Add onions and sauté until clear and beginning to brown. Layer onions, two-thirds of the cheese, and pepper in a greased 2-quart casserole. Set aside. In a saucepan, combine soup, milk, and soy sauce. Heat and stir until well blended. Pour soup mixture over onions and stir gently. Top with French bread slices. Bake at 350° for 15 minutes. Remove from oven and carefully press bread slices into casserole until sauce covers bread. Sprinkle with remaining cheese and return to oven for 15 minutes.
Yield: 8 servings

Chive Mashed Potatoes

2½ POUNDS POTATOES, ABOUT 8 MEDIUM, PEELED AND
CUT INTO 1-INCH CUBES

1 (8 OUNCE) PACKAGE CREAM CHEESE, CUBED AND SOFTENED

¾ TO 1 CUP MILK

½ CUP SNIPPED FRESH CHIVES

1¼ TEASPOONS SALT

¼ TEASPOON BLACK PEPPER

Boil potatoes, covered, in a medium saucepan in 2 inches water for 10 to 12 minutes or until tender; drain. Return to pan and mash with electric mixer or potato masher, gradually stirring in cream cheese until blended. Blend in milk, chives, salt, and pepper. Stir gently over medium heat until heated through. Serve immediately.

Yield: 8 servings

Create a wonderful enhancement for your meals. Soften a stick of real butter to room temperature. Mince ¼ cup of fresh herb of your choice (basil, chive, oregano, rosemary, thyme). Blend the butter and herb, and store in an airtight container. Enjoy with breads and vegetables for up to three weeks.

Creamy Corn Casserole

3 TABLESPOONS BUTTER OR MARGARINE, DIVIDED

1 CUP FINELY CHOPPED CELERY

¼ CUP FINELY CHOPPED ONION

¼ CUP FINELY CHOPPED RED PEPPER

1 (10¾ OUNCE) CAN CONDENSED CREAM OF CHICKEN SOUP

3 CUPS FRESH, FROZEN, OR CANNED CORN, DRAINED

1 (8 OUNCE) CAN SLICED WATER CHESTNUTS, DRAINED

½ CUP SOFT BREAD CRUMBS

Melt 2 tablespoons butter in medium skillet. Add celery, onion, and red pepper and sauté until vegetables are tender, about 2 minutes. Remove from heat and stir in soup, corn, and water chestnuts. Spoon into a greased 2-quart casserole dish. Toss bread crumbs with remaining 1 tablespoon melted butter. Sprinkle on top of casserole and bake, uncovered, at 350° for 25 to 30 minutes.
Yield: 8 servings

Easy Cinnamon Apples

8 TART APPLES, CORED AND SLICED

2 TABLESPOONS SUGAR

1 TEASPOON LEMON JUICE

¼ CUP RED CINNAMON CANDIES

Place all ingredients in a microwave-safe bowl. Heat on high power for 15 minutes, stirring every 5 minutes. May be served warm or cool.
Yield: 8 servings

A simple holiday tablecloth and special napkin rings are fuss-free ways to liven up your dining room for the holiday season.

English Pea Casserole

½ CUP CHOPPED ONION

1 SMALL SWEET RED PEPPER, CHOPPED

¼ CUP BUTTER OR MARGARINE, MELTED

1 (5 OUNCE) PACKAGE MEDIUM EGG NOODLES

1 (8 OUNCE) PACKAGE CREAM CHEESE, SOFTENED

2 CUPS (8 OUNCES) SHREDDED SHARP CHEDDAR CHEESE

1 (10 OUNCE) PACKAGE FROZEN ENGLISH PEAS, THAWED AND DRAINED

1 (2½ OUNCE) JAR MUSHROOM STEMS AND PIECES, UNDRAINED

½ TEASPOON BLACK PEPPER

10 BUTTER-FLAVORED CRACKERS, CRUSHED

In a small skillet, sauté onion and red pepper in butter until tender. Set aside. Cook noodles according to package directions; drain. Add cream cheese and cheddar cheese to hot noodles; stir until cheeses melt. Stir in onion mixture, peas, mushrooms, and pepper. Spoon into a greased baking dish and top with cracker crumbs. Cover and bake at 325° for 25 to 30 minutes.
Yield: 8 servings

Festive Cauliflower

1 LARGE HEAD CAULIFLOWER

2 CUPS WATER

½ TEASPOON SALT

1 TABLESPOON MINCED ONION

1 TABLESPOON MINCED GREEN
PEPPER

1 TABLESPOON MINCED SWEET
RED PEPPER

4 TABLESPOONS BUTTER OR
MARGARINE, DIVIDED

3 TABLESPOONS FLOUR

1 CUP MILK

1 CUP (4 OUNCES) SHREDDED
CHEDDAR CHEESE

¼ TEASPOON DRY MUSTARD

1 DASH GROUND WHITE PEPPER

2 SLICES BACON, COOKED AND
CRUMBLED

1 TABLESPOON SLICED NATURAL
ALMONDS, TOASTED

Remove and discard outer leaves and stalk of cauliflower. Wash cauliflower well, leaving head whole. Place cauliflower in a large saucepan; add water and salt. Bring to a boil; cover, reduce heat to medium, and cook for 10 to 12 minutes or until tender. Drain well. Place cauliflower on a serving platter and keep warm.

Sauté onion and green and red pepper in 1 tablespoon butter in a skillet until tender; drain well and set aside. Melt remaining 3 tablespoons butter in a heavy saucepan over low heat; add flour, stirring until smooth. Cook for 1 minute, stirring constantly. Gradually add milk; cook over medium heat, stirring constantly, until mixture is thickened and bubbly. Add shredded cheese, dry mustard, and ground white pepper, stirring until cheese melts. Remove from heat; stir in reserved vegetable mixture. Spoon sauce over cauliflower. Sprinkle with crumbled bacon and toasted almond slices. Serve immediately.

Yield: 6 servings

French-Style Green Beans

⅔ CUP SLIVERED ALMONDS

6 TABLESPOONS BUTTER OR MARGARINE

2 (10 OUNCE) PACKAGES FROZEN FRENCH-STYLE GREEN BEANS, THAWED

½ TEASPOON SALT

In a large skillet, sauté almonds in butter until lightly browned, about 1 to 2 minutes. Stir in beans and salt; cook and stir for 1 to 2 minutes or until heated through.
Yield: 8 servings

Fruited Wild Rice

1 (6 OUNCE) PACKAGE LONG-GRAIN AND WILD RICE MIX

2 CUPS WATER

1 TABLESPOON BUTTER OR MARGARINE

2 TEASPOONS GRATED ORANGE PEEL, DIVIDED

¼ CUP HALVED GREEN GRAPES

¼ CUP CHOPPED RED DELICIOUS APPLE

¼ CUP GOLDEN RAISINS

¼ CUP SLIVERED ALMONDS, TOASTED

Combine rice mix, water, butter, and 1 teaspoon grated orange peel in a medium saucepan. Bring to a boil; cover, reduce heat, and simmer for 20 to 25 minutes or until rice is tender and liquid is absorbed. Combine grapes, apple, raisins, almonds, and remaining 1 teaspoon orange peel in a large bowl; stir gently. Add rice mixture; toss gently to combine. Serve immediately.

Yield: 6 servings

Ginger Carrots

1½ POUNDS CARROTS, PARED AND SLICED

1 CUP CHICKEN BROTH

**1 (3-INCH) PIECE FRESH GINGER, PEELED AND
CUT INTO ¼-INCH SLICES**

1 TABLESPOON BUTTER

1 DASH RED PEPPER FLAKES

2 TABLESPOONS HONEY

1 GARLIC CLOVE, MINCED

Combine all ingredients in a medium saucepan. Bring to a boil; reduce heat and simmer carrots, uncovered, for 10 to 15 minutes or until carrots are soft and evenly glazed.
Yield: 8 servings

Dried fruit is a wonderful holiday garnish—and decoration. Lay sliced apples (dipped in lemon juice) and oranges on a baking sheet and place in a 200° oven for 2 to 8 hours, turning every hour. If browning starts to occur, remove the slices from the oven or they will quickly scorch. Fruit should be bendable but not sticky. You may also make 6 to 8 slices into the rind of a whole orange or lemon and bake the whole fruit at 200° until completely dried.

Green Bean Bundles

2 (15 OUNCE) CANS WHOLE GREEN BEANS, DRAINED

1 CUP ITALIAN SALAD DRESSING

9 SLICES BACON, CUT IN HALF

In a medium bowl, combine green beans and dressing; toss gently. Cover; chill overnight.

When ready to prepare, preheat oven to 375°. Drain beans; arrange in bundles of 10 to 12 beans each. Wrap half a slice of bacon around each bundle; secure with a toothpick. Bake for 30 minutes or until bacon is done. Yield: 8 to 10 servings

Green Onion and Bacon Mashed Potatoes

4 TO 5 LARGE BAKING POTATOES, PEELED AND CUBED

2 CUPS SHREDDED SHARP CHEDDAR CHEESE

6 BACON SLICES, COOKED AND CRUMBLED, DIVIDED

4 GREEN ONIONS, CHOPPED

2 GARLIC CLOVES, PRESSED

½ CUP SOUR CREAM

¼ CUP BUTTER OR MARGARINE, SOFTENED

1½ TEASPOONS SALT

½ TEASPOON BLACK PEPPER

Place potatoes in a large Dutch oven and cover with water; bring to a boil and cook for 25 minutes or until tender. Drain. Mash potatoes; stir in cheese, three-quarters of the crumbled bacon, onions, garlic, sour cream, butter, salt, and pepper. Sprinkle ¼ cup crumbled bacon on top. Serve immediately.

Yield: 6 to 8 servings

A great way to warm hearts on cold winter days is to tell your loved ones how much they mean to you. That, along with a steaming mug of hot chocolate, can't be beat!

Above all, love each other deeply.

1 PETER 4:8

Mariann's Stuffing Balls

2 (1 POUND) LOAVES BREAD

2 STALKS CELERY, FINELY CHOPPED

1 SMALL TO MEDIUM ONION, FINELY CHOPPED

½ CUP BUTTER

2 EGGS, SLIGHTLY BEATEN

⅛ TO ¼ TEASPOON POULTRY SEASONING

GARLIC POWDER TO TASTE

FRESHLY GROUND BLACK PEPPER TO TASTE

1 (10¾ OUNCE) CAN CONDENSED CREAM OF CHICKEN SOUP

1 (15 OUNCE) CAN CHICKEN BROTH

1 PACKET CHICKEN GRAVY MIX

Roast bread in a 200° oven until thoroughly dried and crusty but not dark. Cool and cube into a very large mixing bowl or roaster pan. Microwave celery, onion, and butter on high power for 2 minutes; stir and microwave for about 2 more minutes until onions look transparent. Cool completely. Mix well with bread cubes. Add beaten eggs to bread and celery mixture, stirring to distribute evenly. Sprinkle in seasonings. Add condensed soup and mix well. Stir chicken broth throughout mixture. Let stand for a few minutes to allow moisture to set in. The mixture should be somewhat wet. Form into 2- to 3-inch balls. Place in a 9 x 13-inch pan sprayed with cooking oil.

Make up gravy mix, adding 1 cup milk instead of water. Cook according to package directions. Spoon over each ball. Cover and bake at 325° for approximately 30 minutes.

Stuffing balls can be made ahead and prebaked without gravy then frozen individually. You can enjoy quick single servings this way. Prepare gravy and spoon over stuffing balls before warming.
Yield: 24 to 26 stuffing balls

Orange-Sweet Potato Casserole

4 LARGE SWEET POTATOES

½ CUP BROWN SUGAR, DIVIDED

2 TABLESPOONS BUTTER OR MARGARINE

1 (11 OUNCE) CAN MANDARIN ORANGES, DRAINED

½ CUP ORANGE JUICE

TOPPING:

½ CUP CHOPPED WALNUTS

¼ CUP SWEETENED, FLAKED COCONUT

1 TABLESPOON BROWN SUGAR

½ TEASPOON GROUND CINNAMON

2 TABLESPOONS BUTTER OR MARGARINE

Boil whole potatoes for 30 to 40 minutes. Cool, then peel and slice into ¼-inch slices. Arrange half of potato slices in a greased casserole. Sprinkle with ¼ cup brown sugar. Dot with butter. Arrange half of the oranges on top. Repeat layers. Pour orange juice over all. Cover and bake at 350° for 45 minutes. While casserole is baking, mix together walnuts, coconut, brown sugar, and cinnamon. Cut butter into mixture and set aside.

Remove casserole from oven, uncover, and sprinkle topping over potatoes. Return to oven uncovered for 10 minutes.

Yield: 8 servings

Oyster Corn Bread Dressing

2 (8 OUNCE) PACKAGES CORN BREAD MIX

4 TABLESPOONS BUTTER

¾ CUP CHOPPED ONION

3 STALKS CELERY, CHOPPED

2 GARLIC CLOVES, MINCED

2 (8 OUNCE) CANS OYSTERS, LIQUID RESERVED AND OYSTERS
CHOPPED (LESS IS ACCEPTABLE, OR SUBSTITUTE ½ TO 1 CUP
TURKEY GIBLETS, COOKED AND CHOPPED)

2 EGGS, BEATEN

½ TEASPOON BLACK PEPPER

1½ TEASPOONS GROUND SAGE

3 TEASPOONS POULTRY SEASONING

1 (14 OUNCE) CAN CHICKEN STOCK

Prepare corn bread as instructed on package; allow to cool before crumbling corn bread into a large mixing bowl. In a large saucepan, melt butter over low heat and sauté onion, celery, garlic, and oysters until onion is glassy and tender. Stir oysters into corn bread crumbs. In a separate bowl, beat eggs; then season with pepper, sage, and poultry seasoning. Mix in chicken stock and reserved oyster liquid. Blend egg mixture into corn bread mixture. Place in a 2-quart casserole that has been sprayed with oil. Bake, uncovered, at 350° for 45 minutes.
Yield: 8 servings

Potluck Potatoes

9 MEDIUM RUSSET POTATOES, PEELED AND CUBED

1 (8 OUNCE) PACKAGE CREAM CHEESE, SOFTENED

2 TABLESPOONS BUTTER OR MARGARINE

½ CUP SOUR CREAM

2 CUPS (8 OUNCES) SHREDDED CHEDDAR CHEESE, DIVIDED

1 TEASPOON GARLIC SALT

1 TEASPOON ONION SALT

**1 (10 OUNCE) PACKAGE FROZEN CHOPPED SPINACH,
THAWED AND SQUEEZED DRY**

Place potatoes in a large saucepan; cover with water. Cover and bring to a boil. Cook for 20 to 25 minutes, until tender. Drain. Transfer to a mixing bowl and mash with cream cheese and butter. Stir in sour cream, 1 cup cheddar cheese, garlic salt, onion salt, and spinach. Spoon into a greased 2-quart baking dish. Bake at 350° for 30 to 35 minutes or until thoroughly heated. Sprinkle with remaining cheese; bake 5 minutes longer or until cheese is melted and bubbly.
Yield: 10 to 12 servings

Rye Stuffing

1 POUND DAY-OLD LIGHT RYE
BREAD, CUBED

$\frac{1}{2}$ POUND DAY-OLD DARK RYE
BREAD, CUBED

1 POUND MILD BULK SAUSAGE

$1\frac{1}{2}$ CUPS CHOPPED ONION

2 LARGE COOKING APPLES, PEELED
AND CHOPPED

1 CUP CHOPPED CELERY

3 GARLIC CLOVES, MINCED

$\frac{1}{2}$ CUP BUTTER OR MARGARINE

$\frac{3}{4}$ CUP CHOPPED PECANS

2 TABLESPOONS DRIED PARSLEY
FLAKES

2 TEASPOONS SALT

2 TEASPOONS GROUND THYME

$1\frac{1}{2}$ TEASPOONS GROUND SAGE

$\frac{3}{4}$ TEASPOON DRIED ROSEMARY,
CRUSHED

$\frac{1}{2}$ TEASPOON BLACK PEPPER

$\frac{1}{4}$ TEASPOON GROUND NUTMEG

3 TO $3\frac{1}{2}$ CUPS CHICKEN BROTH

Combine bread cubes in a large bowl. In a skillet, cook and crumble
sausage; drain. To same skillet, add onion, apples, celery, garlic, and butter.
Sauté until apples and vegetables are tender. Add onion mixture and
sausage to bread. Add pecans, seasonings, and enough broth to moisten.
Cover and refrigerate until ready to bake.

Stuff turkey just before baking and bake according to package directions, or spoon stuffing into a greased 9 x 13-inch baking dish and bake at
325° for 1 hour.
Yield: 10 to 12 servings

*I like crispy dressing—and I like neat serving
portions. I've baked up dressing recipes in muffin
tins. A pan of dressing muffins will bake at 350°
for 15 to 20 minutes and make perfectly
portioned servings for your feast.*

Slow-Cooker Stuffing

2 TABLESPOONS BUTTER OR MARGARINE

1 CUP SLICED FRESH MUSHROOMS

1 CUP CHOPPED CELERY

1 CUP CHOPPED ONION

10 CUPS DAY-OLD BREAD CUBES

¼ CUP BUTTER

1 TABLESPOON CHICKEN BOUILLON POWDER

1½ CUPS HOT WATER

1 TEASPOON DRIED PARSLEY FLAKES

2 TEASPOONS POULTRY SEASONING

1 TEASPOON SALT

1 TEASPOON BLACK PEPPER

Melt butter in a skillet. Sauté mushrooms, celery, and onion. Pour over bread crumbs in a large bowl. Place butter and bouillon powder in a small bowl. Pour hot water over mixture and stir to melt butter and dissolve powder. Pour over bread mixture. Add remaining seasonings and toss to coat. Turn into a lightly greased slow cooker; cover and cook on low for 6 hours.
Yield: 8 servings

Twice-Baked Sweet Potatoes

6 MEDIUM SWEET POTATOES

2 TABLESPOONS BUTTER, SOFTENED

½ CUP ORANGE JUICE

1 (8 OUNCE) CAN CRUSHED PINEAPPLE, DRAINED

2 TABLESPOONS BROWN SUGAR

Pierce sweet potatoes with a fork. Bake at 400° until tender, 45 to 60 minutes. Let potatoes cool slightly. Cut a thin slice off the top of each potato and scoop out pulp, leaving a thin shell. In a large bowl, mash potato pulp; stir in butter, orange juice, and pineapple. Refill potato shells. Sprinkle with brown sugar. Bake at 400° for 15 to 20 minutes, until heated through.
Yield: 6 servings

Use three-ring binders to create family cookbooks. Include recipes for all the family favorites with a brief bio and photo of the creator of each dish. These gifts will be cherished for years to come.

Two-Cheese Broccoli Casserole

2 TABLESPOONS BUTTER OR MARGARINE

2 TABLESPOONS FLOUR

1 CUP MILK

3 OUNCES CREAM CHEESE, SOFTENED

¼ CUP BLUE CHEESE, CRUMBLED

2 (10 OUNCE) PACKAGES FROZEN CHOPPED BROCCOLI

½ CUP SOFT BREAD CRUMBS

Melt butter in a saucepan. Stir in flour and cook for 1 minute. Gradually add milk and continue cooking, stirring constantly, until thickened and bubbly. Add cheeses; cook until cheese melts and mixture is smooth. Cook broccoli according to package directions; drain. Stir cheese mixture into broccoli. Turn into a buttered ½-quart casserole dish. Sprinkle with bread crumbs and bake, uncovered, at 350° for 30 minutes.
Yield: 6 servings

Zesty Carrots

6 TO 8 CARROTS, CUT INTO ¼-INCH SLICES

½ CUP MAYONNAISE

2 TABLESPOONS MINCED ONION

1 TABLESPOON PREPARED HORSERADISH

¼ CUP SHREDDED CHEDDAR CHEESE

1 TEASPOON SALT

¼ TEASPOON BLACK PEPPER

½ CUP CRUSHED CORNFLAKES

1 TABLESPOON BUTTER OR MARGARINE, MELTED

Place carrots in a saucepan and cover with water. Cook for 5 minutes. Drain, reserving ¼ cup water. Pour reserved liquid into mixing bowl. Stir in mayonnaise, onion, horseradish, cheese, salt, and pepper. Mix well. Add carrots; transfer to a greased 2-quart casserole. Sprinkle with crushed cornflakes and drizzle with butter. Bake at 350° for 20 to 25 minutes. Yield: 8 servings

SALADS

Ambrosia

3 (15 OUNCE) CANS FRUIT COCKTAIL, DRAINED

1 (11 OUNCE) CAN MANDARIN ORANGES, DRAINED

1 CUP MINIATURE MARSHMALLOWS

1 CUP SWEETENED, FLAKED COCONUT

2 BANANAS, SLICED

1 JAR MARASCHINO CHERRIES, DRAINED AND HALVED

1 (5 OUNCE) CAN EVAPORATED MILK

Combine all ingredients in a large bowl. Refrigerate for at least 1 hour before serving.
Yield: 6 servings

Candy Apple Salad

2 CUPS WATER

¼ CUP RED CINNAMON CANDIES

1 (3 OUNCE) PACKAGE CHERRY GELATIN

½ CUP CHOPPED CELERY

1½ CUPS CHOPPED TART APPLES

½ CUP CHOPPED WALNUTS

In a saucepan, bring water to a boil. Add in cinnamon candies; stir until dissolved. Remove from heat and add gelatin; stir until dissolved. Cool slightly, then refrigerate until gelatin begins to thicken. Add remaining ingredients; blend well. Pour into 8-inch square dish and chill until firm. Yield: 6 servings

Champagne Salad

1 (8 OUNCE) PACKAGE CREAM CHEESE, SOFTENED

¾ CUP SUGAR

1 (20 OUNCE) CAN CRUSHED PINEAPPLE, DRAINED

1 (10 OUNCE) PACKAGE FROZEN STRAWBERRIES, WITH JUICE

2 BANANAS, SLICED

½ CUP CHOPPED NUTS

1 (16 OUNCE) CONTAINER FROZEN WHIPPED TOPPING, THAWED

Beat cream cheese with sugar. In a separate bowl, mix together pineapple, strawberries with juice, bananas, nuts, and whipped topping. Gently combine with cream cheese mixture. Pour into a 9 x 13-inch pan and freeze completely. To serve, thaw slightly and cut into squares. Keep leftovers frozen.
Yield: 12 to 16 servings

When a recipe calls for 2 cups of whipped topping, I sometimes like to increase the quality and flavor by using whipping cream. 1 cup of whipping cream, whipped, equals 2 cups of frozen whipped topping.

Christmas Crunch Salad

1½ CUPS BROCCOLI FLORETS

1½ CUPS CAULIFLOWER FLORETS

1 RED ONION, CHOPPED

2 CUPS CHERRY TOMATOES, CUT IN HALF

DRESSING:

1 CUP MAYONNAISE

½ CUP SOUR CREAM

1 TABLESPOON VINEGAR

2 TABLESPOONS SUGAR

SALT AND PEPPER TO TASTE

Combine vegetables in a large bowl. Set aside. In a small bowl, whisk together dressing ingredients. Pour over vegetables and gently stir to coat. Chill for at least 2 hours before serving.
Yield: 6 servings

Looking for a simple but pretty holiday centerpiece for your dining room table? Fill a glass bowl with snowflake- or other holiday-shaped confetti along with some candy canes. A glass bowl filled with colored bulb ornaments makes for a festive centerpiece, too.

Christmas Fruit Salad

3 EGG YOLKS, BEATEN

3 TABLESPOONS WATER

3 TABLESPOONS WHITE VINEGAR

½ TEASPOON SALT

2 CUPS WHIPPING CREAM, WHIPPED

3 CUPS MINIATURE MARSHMALLOWS

2 CUPS SEEDLESS GREEN GRAPES, HALVED

1 (20 OUNCE) CAN PINEAPPLE TIDBITS, DRAINED

1 (11 OUNCE) CAN MANDARIN ORANGES, DRAINED

1 (10 OUNCE) JAR RED MARASCHINO CHERRIES, DRAINED AND SLICED

1 CUP CHOPPED PECANS

3 TABLESPOONS LEMON JUICE

In a large saucepan, combine egg yolks, water, vinegar, and salt. Stirring constantly, cook over medium heat until mixture thickens. Remove from heat and fold in whipped cream. In a large bowl, mix together remaining ingredients. Add dressing and stir gently to combine. Cover and refrigerate overnight.

Yield: 12 to 14 servings

Cranberry Salad

1 (3 OUNCE) PACKAGE CHERRY GELATIN

1 CUP HOT WATER

1 CAN WHOLE BERRY CRANBERRY SAUCE

1 CUP SOUR CREAM

½ CUP CHOPPED PECANS

Mix gelatin with hot water. Stir until dissolved. Refrigerate until slightly congealed. Stir in cranberry sauce, sour cream, and pecans. Pour into a mold and refrigerate until completely set.

Yield: 4 to 6 servings

European Salad

DRESSING:

1 CUP RICE VINEGAR

½ CUP WINE VINEGAR

4 TABLESPOONS SUGAR

3 GARLIC CLOVES, MINCED

SALT AND PEPPER TO TASTE

1 CUP CANOLA OIL

SALAD:

8 CUPS SPRING SALAD MIX

¾ CUP CHOPPED GREEN ONIONS

½ RED ONION, CHOPPED

6 OUNCES FETA CHEESE, CRUMBLED

1 CUP DRIED CRANBERRIES

1 CUP SLICED FRESH MUSHROOMS

3 HARD-BOILED EGGS, SLICED

1 CUP TOASTED PINE NUTS

Prepare dressing the night before salad is to be served. Whisk together vinegars, sugar, garlic, and salt and pepper. Gradually whisk in oil. Chill. The following day, toss salad ingredients in a serving bowl. Drizzle dressing over salad just before serving. Toss to coat.
Yield: 8 to 10 servings

Frog Eye Salad

1 CUP SUGAR

3 EGG YOLKS

2 TABLESPOONS FLOUR

2 CUPS PINEAPPLE JUICE

1 TABLESPOON LEMON JUICE

1 (16 OUNCE) PACKAGE ACINI DI PEPE PASTA

2 (20 OUNCE) CANS PINEAPPLE CHUNKS, DRAINED

2 (11 OUNCE) CANS MANDARIN ORANGES, DRAINED

1 (16 OUNCE) PACKAGE MINIATURE MARSHMALLOWS

1 (12 OUNCE) CONTAINER FROZEN WHIPPED TOPPING, THAWED

In a large saucepan over low heat, whisk together sugar, egg yolks, flour, pineapple juice, and lemon juice. Cook and stir until thickened. Remove from heat. Meanwhile, bring a large pot of lightly salted water to a boil. Add pasta and cook for 8 to 10 minutes or until al dente; drain and rinse with cold water. In a large bowl, combine cooked mixture with pasta and gently stir to combine. Refrigerate at least 4 hours or overnight. When chilled, toss pasta with pineapple chunks, mandarin oranges, marshmallows, and whipped topping. Refrigerate until ready to serve.
Yield: 12 servings

Fruity Cranberry Salad

2 CUPS FRESH OR FROZEN CRANBERRIES

1 MEDIUM UNPEELED ORANGE, QUARTERED AND SEEDED

¾ CUP SUGAR

1 (3 OUNCE) PACKAGE CHERRY GELATIN

1 CUP BOILING WATER

1 CUP SEEDLESS RED GRAPES, HALVED

1 CUP CRUSHED PINEAPPLE, WELL DRAINED

½ CUP CHOPPED CELERY

¼ CUP FINELY CHOPPED PECANS

In food processor, combine first three ingredients. Cover and process until fruit is coarsely chopped. Set aside for 30 minutes. Meanwhile, dissolve gelatin in boiling water. Chill until gelatin begins to thicken. Stir in cranberry mixture, grapes, pineapple, celery, and pecans. Pour into a serving bowl and refrigerate overnight.
Yield: 12 servings

Holiday Slaw

1 (1 POUND) PACKAGE BROCCOLI SLAW MIX

⅔ CUP RAISINS

¾ CUP COARSELY CHOPPED WALNUTS OR PECANS

1 LARGE APPLE, CHOPPED

1 CUP PREPARED POPPY SEED DRESSING

In a large bowl, combine first four ingredients. Pour prepared dressing over mixture and stir gently until evenly coated. Chill for 2 to 3 hours to blend flavors before serving.
Yield: 8 servings

Hot Fruit Salad

1 (29 OUNCE) CAN SLICED PEACHES, PARTIALLY DRAINED

1 (20 OUNCE) CAN PINEAPPLE CHUNKS, PARTIALLY DRAINED

1 CUP FRESH CRANBERRIES

¾ CUP BROWN SUGAR

2 TABLESPOONS MINUTE TAPIOCA

BUTTER

GROUND CINNAMON

Mix together peaches, pineapple chunks, cranberries, brown sugar, and tapioca. Spoon into a greased casserole. Dot with butter and sprinkle with cinnamon. Bake, covered, at 350° for 30 minutes. Stir; bake, uncovered, for 15 minutes longer. Serve warm.
Yield: 6 servings

This Christmas, clear your mind of all the clutter. Forget about having a spotless house. Forget about shopping. Forget about having the perfect decorations. Forget about planning the perfect holiday menu. Instead, take time to focus on God's Gift of Hope He sent on that silent night so long ago.

"She will give birth to a son, and you are to give him the name Jesus, because he will save his people from their sins."

MATTHEW 1:21

Layered Broccoli-Cauliflower Salad

6 SLICES BACON

1 CUP BROCCOLI FLORETS

1 CUP CAULIFLOWER FLORETS

3 HARD-BOILED EGGS, CHOPPED

½ CUP CHOPPED RED ONION

1 CUP MAYONNAISE

½ CUP SUGAR

2 TABLESPOONS WHITE WINE VINEGAR

1 CUP SHREDDED CHEDDAR CHEESE

In a large skillet, cook bacon over medium-high heat until crispy. Crumble and set aside. In a medium glass salad bowl, layer in order the broccoli, cauliflower, eggs, and onion. Prepare dressing by whisking together mayonnaise, sugar, and vinegar. Drizzle dressing over top. Sprinkle crumbled bacon and cheese over dressing. Chill completely to blend flavors. Yield: 8 servings

Mandarin Orange Salad

2 CUPS BOILING WATER

1 (6 OUNCE) PACKAGE ORANGE GELATIN

1 PINT ORANGE SHERBET

1 (11 OUNCE) CAN MANDARIN ORANGES, DRAINED

1 (8½ OUNCE) CAN CRUSHED PINEAPPLE, UNDRAINED

In a mixing bowl, pour boiling water over gelatin. Stir until dissolved.
Spoon orange sherbet into gelatin and stir until well combined. Fold in
remaining ingredients. Pour into a gelatin mold and refrigerate until firm.
Yield: 8 servings

Marinated Vegetable Salad

¾ CUP WHITE VINEGAR

½ CUP OIL

1 CUP SUGAR

1 TEASPOON SALT

½ TEASPOON BLACK PEPPER

2 (11 OUNCE) CANS WHITE CORN

1 (15 OUNCE) CAN SMALL SWEET PEAS

1 (15 OUNCE) CAN FRENCH-STYLE GREEN BEANS

1 CUP DICED GREEN PEPPER

1 CUP DICED CELERY

1 CUP DICED ONION

1 (2 OUNCE) JAR DICED PIMIENTO

In a small saucepan, bring vinegar, oil, sugar, salt, and pepper to a boil; stir until sugar dissolves. Cool. Combine remaining ingredients in a bowl. Stir in vinegar mixture. Chill for 8 hours or overnight. Drain before serving. Yield: 10 to 12 servings

Merry Vegetable Salad

1 (16 OUNCE) CAN WHOLE-KERNEL CORN, DRAINED

1 LARGE TOMATO, SEEDED AND CHOPPED

1 CUP FROZEN PEAS

½ CUP CHOPPED CELERY

⅓ CUP CHOPPED GREEN PEPPER

¼ CUP CHOPPED RED PEPPER

¼ CUP FINELY CHOPPED ONION

DRESSING:

¼ CUP SOUR CREAM

2 TABLESPOONS MAYONNAISE

2 TEASPOONS WHITE VINEGAR

¼ TEASPOON SALT

⅛ TEASPOON BLACK PEPPER

Combine vegetables. In a small bowl, whisk together dressing ingredients.
Just before serving, add dressing to vegetables and toss to coat.
Yield: 6 to 8 servings

Minestrone Salad

4 OUNCES UNCOOKED ANGEL HAIR PASTA, BROKEN INTO 2-INCH PIECES

1 CUP JULIENNED CARROTS

¼ CUP CHOPPED FRESH PARSLEY

3 MEDIUM ROMA TOMATOES, SEEDED AND CHOPPED

1 CUP JULIENNED ZUCCHINI

1 (15 OUNCE) CAN GARBANZO BEANS, RINSED AND DRAINED

1 (6 OUNCE) JAR MARINATED ARTICHOKE HEARTS,
DRAINED, LIQUID RESERVED

1 CUP MOZZARELLA CHEESE, CUT INTO ½-INCH CUBES

DRESSING:

RESERVED ARTICHOKE LIQUID

2 TABLESPOONS CIDER VINEGAR

½ TEASPOON GARLIC SALT

⅛ TEASPOON BLACK PEPPER

Cook pasta according to package directions. Rinse with cold water; drain and set aside.

Meanwhile, in a medium saucepan, combine carrots and enough water to cover. Bring to a full boil and continue cooking until carrots are crisp-tender (1 to 2 minutes). Rinse with cold water; drain. In a large bowl, combine pasta, carrots, parsley, tomatoes, zucchini, beans, drained artichokes, and cheese.

In a small jar with a tight-fitting lid, combine reserved artichoke liquid, vinegar, garlic salt, and pepper; shake well to blend. Pour dressing over salad; toss to coat. Cover; refrigerate at least 2 hours before serving.
Yield: 6 servings

Nutty Pear Salad

2 CANS (45 OUNCES TOTAL) PEAR HALVES

LEMON JUICE

1 (8 OUNCE) PACKAGE CREAM CHEESE, SOFTENED

1 TABLESPOON SUGAR

¼ CUP CHOPPED WALNUTS

MARASCHINO CHERRIES, HALVED

Drain pear halves, reserving 1 tablespoon syrup. Brush each pear with lemon juice. In a small bowl, beat cream cheese, sugar, and reserved syrup until smooth. Fold in walnuts. Spoon mixture into each pear half. Top with a halved maraschino cherry.
Yield: 8 servings

Buy some spring bulbs for daffodils, tulips, or hyacinths, and put them in the coldest corner of your refrigerator for 2 to 4 weeks. Fill over half a bucket or large vase with gravel, pebbles, or marbles. Nestle the bulbs among the top pebbles, points facing upward. Add water just to the tops of the pebbles. In a few weeks there will be blossoms for all to enjoy. Give them away at any stage of growth.

Orange Sherbet Salad

2 (3 OUNCE) PACKAGES ORANGE GELATIN

1 CUP BOILING WATER

1 CUP ORANGE JUICE

1 PINT ORANGE SHERBET

1 (11 OUNCE) CAN MANDARIN ORANGES, DRAINED AND CUT UP

1 (8 OUNCE) CAN CRUSHED PINEAPPLE, DRAINED

2 BANANAS, PEELED AND SLICED

1 CUP SOUR CREAM

1 CUP MINIATURE MARSHMALLOWS

Dissolve gelatin in boiling water; add orange juice and sherbet. Stir until sherbet is melted. Add fruit; chill until firm. In a small bowl, combine sour cream and marshmallows; spread over top of salad just before serving. Yield: 10 servings

Oriental Ramen Noodle Salad

2 TABLESPOONS BUTTER OR MARGARINE

1 (3 OUNCE) PACKAGE ORIENTAL-FLAVOR RAMEN NOODLE SOUP,
SEASONING PACKET RESERVED

½ CUP SLICED ALMONDS

⅔ CUP EVAPORATED MILK

⅔ CUP VEGETABLE OIL

3 TABLESPOONS WHITE VINEGAR

2 TABLESPOONS SUGAR

2 (10 OUNCE) PACKAGES ROMAINE-RADICCHIO LETTUCE

2 GREEN ONIONS, THINLY SLICED

1 (10 OUNCE) CAN MANDARIN ORANGES, DRAINED

Melt butter in a large skillet. Crumble ramen noodles and add to skillet
with almonds; cook, stirring constantly, until noodles are golden. Remove
from pan; cool completely and set aside. In blender, combine evaporated
milk, oil, vinegar, ramen seasoning packet, and sugar. Cover and blend until
smooth.

Combine salad greens, noodle mixture, green onions, oranges, and
dressing in a large bowl; toss to coat. Serve immediately.
Yield: 8 servings

Pink Salad

1 (24 OUNCE) CARTON COTTAGE CHEESE

1 (3 OUNCE) PACKAGE STRAWBERRY GELATIN

1 (8 OUNCE) CARTON FROZEN WHIPPED TOPPING, THAWED

½ CUP MINIATURE MARSHMALLOWS

½ CUP NUTS (OPTIONAL)

Mix cottage cheese and gelatin. Gently fold in whipped topping and marshmallows. Stir in nuts if desired. Spoon into serving dish and chill until set.
Yield: 8 servings

Sauerkraut Salad

1 (27 OUNCE) CAN SAUERKRAUT, DRAINED AND RINSED

1 LARGE SWEET ONION, CHOPPED

1 GREEN PEPPER, CHOPPED

1 CUP CHOPPED CELERY

2 TEASPOONS DICED PIMIENTO

1 CUP SUGAR

½ CUP SALAD OIL

½ CUP WHITE VINEGAR

In a large bowl, mix together sauerkraut, onion, green pepper, celery, and pimiento. In a small bowl, whisk together sugar, oil, and vinegar. Pour oil and vinegar mixture over vegetables and mix to coat. Chill thoroughly. Yield: 8 to 10 servings

I praise You, Lord. You alone are all I need to melt away the stresses of the holiday. Amen.

Strawberry-Orange Salad

2 (3 OUNCE) PACKAGES STRAWBERRY GELATIN

2 CUPS BOILING WATER

1 (10 OUNCE) PACKAGE FROZEN STRAWBERRIES,
THAWED AND DRAINED, JUICE RESERVED

$\frac{1}{3}$ CUP ORANGE JUICE

1 (11 OUNCE) CAN MANDARIN ORANGES, DRAINED

$\frac{1}{3}$ CUP SOUR CREAM

In a large bowl, pour boiling water over gelatin; stir until gelatin is dissolved. Combine reserved strawberry juice and orange juice in a small bowl; stir into gelatin. Reserve 1 tablespoon mixture; set aside. Cover gelatin mixture and chill until slightly thickened. Gently stir in strawberries and oranges. Pour into a gelatin mold. Cover and refrigerate until set.

Meanwhile, blend sour cream and reserved gelatin mixture in a small bowl. Cover; refrigerate until serving time. Serve sour cream mixture with salad.

Yield: 8 servings

Strawberry Pretzel Salad

¾ CUP BUTTER OR MARGARINE, MELTED

3 TABLESPOONS SUGAR

2 CUPS CRUSHED PRETZELS

1 (8 OUNCE) PACKAGE CREAM CHEESE, SOFTENED

¾ CUP SUGAR

1 (8 OUNCE) CARTON FROZEN WHIPPED TOPPING, THAWED

2 (3 OUNCE) PACKAGES STRAWBERRY GELATIN

2 CUPS BOILING WATER

1 (16 OUNCE) PACKAGE FROZEN STRAWBERRIES

1 (8 OUNCE) CAN CRUSHED PINEAPPLE, DRAINED

Mix butter, 3 tablespoons sugar, and crushed pretzels; then press mixture into a 9 x 13-inch pan. Bake at 350° for 10 minutes. Cool completely. In a mixing bowl, beat cream cheese with ¾ cup sugar. Fold in whipped topping. Spread evenly over cooled pretzel crust. Combine gelatin with boiling water. Stir to dissolve. Mix in frozen strawberries and pineapple. Allow gelatin to set slightly. Pour gelatin over cheese mixture. Refrigerate until completely set. Yield: 12 to 15 servings

Feed the birds, too—don't forget the wild birds on those snowy Christmas days. Spread peanut butter on a pinecone; then roll it in bird seed. Use a wire to hang it on a tree. You can also cut an orange in half, scoop out the fruit, and fill the rind cup with bird seed. It can be fashioned into a basket that will hang from a tree limb.

Tortellini Salad

1 (9 OUNCE) PACKAGE FROZEN CHEESE TORTELLINI

1 (10 OUNCE) PACKAGE TRI-COLORED ROTINI

1 (6 OUNCE) PACKAGE SALAMI, CHOPPED

1 (10¾ OUNCE) CAN SLICED BLACK OLIVES, DRAINED

1 CUP SLICED GREEN OLIVES

1 GREEN PEPPER, CHOPPED

1 CUP CHOPPED CUCUMBER

½ CUP CHOPPED CELERY

1 CUP ITALIAN DRESSING

1 DASH SALT

1 DASH PEPPER

1 DASH GARLIC SALT

FRESHLY GRATED PARMESAN CHEESE

Cook tortellini and rotini according to package directions. Drain. Rinse with cold water; combine pastas in a large bowl. Add salami, black olives, green olives, green pepper, cucumber, and celery to pasta. In a small bowl, whisk together Italian dressing, salt, pepper, and garlic salt. Pour dressing over salad ingredients and toss to coat. Top with grated Parmesan cheese. Yield: 12 to 16 servings

Wilted Spinach Salad

8 SLICES BACON, DICED

1 TABLESPOON BROWN SUGAR

⅓ CUP THINLY SLICED GREEN ONIONS

SALT TO TASTE

3 TABLESPOONS WHITE VINEGAR

¼ TEASPOON DRY MUSTARD

1 POUND FRESH SPINACH, WASHED, DRIED, AND CHILLED

1 HARD-BOILED EGG, CHOPPED

In a heavy skillet, fry diced bacon until crisp. Reduce heat; stir in brown sugar, onions, salt, vinegar, and mustard; bring to a boil. Pour hot mixture over spinach. Toss lightly. Sprinkle chopped egg over salad. Serve immediately.
Yield: 6 servings

SKIPPIN' THE MISTLETOE

And Headin' Straight for the Desserts!

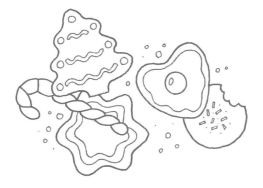

The dessert crowns the dinner.

Eugene Briffault (1799–1854), author of *Paris a Table*

COOKIES

Ana Lisa Cookies

1½ CUPS BUTTER

1 CUP SUGAR

1 EGG

1 TEASPOON ALMOND EXTRACT

3¼ CUPS SIFTED FLOUR

LINGONBERRIES

CHOPPED ALMONDS

GLAZE:

2½ CUPS POWDERED SUGAR

2 TABLESPOONS WATER

1 TABLESPOON BUTTER, SOFTENED

1 TABLESPOON LIGHT CORN SYRUP

½ TEASPOON ALMOND EXTRACT

Cream butter with sugar. Add egg and almond extract; mix well. Stir in flour until completely blended. Refrigerate at least 4 hours or overnight.

Roll out dough about ⅜ inch thick. Using two round cookie cutters (one smaller), cut circular shapes. Place larger circles on ungreased cookie sheets. Place a small amount of berries in the center of each circle. Use smaller circles to cover filling. Gently press around the edges, keeping filling inside. Bake at 375° for 6 to 8 minutes. Cool completely.

For glaze, combine powdered sugar, water, butter, corn syrup, and almond extract in a small mixing bowl; mix until powdered sugar is moistened. Beat at medium speed until smooth, adding additional water if necessary to reach desired glazing consistency.
Yield: 2 dozen cookies

Belgian Christmas Bars

1⅔ CUPS FLOUR

1½ TEASPOONS BAKING POWDER

½ TEASPOON SALT

⅔ CUP VEGETABLE SHORTENING

1 CUP BROWN SUGAR, PACKED

2 LARGE EGGS

1 TEASPOON ALMOND EXTRACT

½ CUP CHOPPED BLANCHED ALMONDS

½ TEASPOON GROUND CINNAMON

RED AND GREEN COLORED SUGAR

Combine flour, baking powder, and salt; set aside. In a large mixing bowl, cream shortening and brown sugar. Beat in eggs and almond extract. Gradually blend in dry ingredients. Spread evenly in an ungreased 9 x 13-inch baking pan. Scatter almonds and cinnamon over top. Sprinkle with colored sugar. Bake at 375° for 10 to 12 minutes or until lightly browned. Cut into bars while still warm.
Yield: 2 dozen bars

Use a stencil or a lacy paper doily to easily decorate cakes, bars, and cookies. Place the stencil on top of a warm cake and sift powdered sugar or cocoa over all. Carefully remove the stencil, and you'll be left with a fantastic design.

Best Peanut Butter Cookies

½ CUP CREAMY PEANUT BUTTER

¼ CUP CRUNCHY PEANUT BUTTER

½ CUP VEGETABLE SHORTENING

1¼ CUPS BROWN SUGAR, PACKED

3 TABLESPOONS MILK

1 TABLESPOON VANILLA EXTRACT

1 EGG

1¾ CUPS FLOUR

¾ TEASPOON SALT

¾ TEASPOON BAKING SODA

Combine peanut butter, shortening, brown sugar, milk, and vanilla in a large mixing bowl. Beat at medium speed until well blended. Add egg. Beat just until blended. Combine flour, salt, and baking soda. Add to creamed mixture at low speed. Mix just until blended. Drop by heaping teaspoonfuls 2 inches apart onto ungreased cookie sheets. Flatten slightly in crisscross pattern with tines of fork. Bake at 375° for 7 to 8 minutes or until set and just beginning to brown. Cool for 2 minutes on baking sheet before transferring to cooling racks to cool completely.
Yield: 3 dozen cookies

For perfect crisscross patterns on top of your peanut butter cookies, first wet the prongs of a table fork with milk. Then dip the fork in white sugar and press into the dough twice, forming a cross design.

Brown Sugar Cutouts

1 CUP BUTTER OR MARGARINE, SOFTENED

½ CUP SUGAR

1 CUP BROWN SUGAR, PACKED

1 LARGE EGG, LIGHTLY BEATEN

½ CUP SOUR CREAM

1 TEASPOON VANILLA EXTRACT

4½ CUPS FLOUR

½ TEASPOON BAKING POWDER

½ TEASPOON BAKING SODA

½ TEASPOON SALT

In a large mixing bowl, cream butter and sugars. Add egg; beat until well blended. Stir in sour cream and vanilla. Combine dry ingredients; add slowly to creamed mixture. Mix well. Refrigerate dough for 1 hour. On lightly floured surface, roll out half of the chilled dough to ¼-inch thickness. Cut with desired cookie cutters and place on lightly greased cookie sheets. Bake at 350° for 10 to 12 minutes.
Yield: 3 to 4 dozen cookies

Host a Christmas cookie–baking marathon. Invite family and friends to bring ingredients for a variety of cookies. Spend all afternoon baking and decorating. Send each participant home with a platter filled with your yummy creations. Definitely much more fun—and simpler—than doing all the work yourself!

Butterscotch Cookies

1 CUP BUTTER OR MARGARINE, SOFTENED

2 CUPS BROWN SUGAR, PACKED

2 EGGS, LIGHTLY BEATEN

1 TEASPOON VANILLA EXTRACT

3½ CUPS FLOUR

½ TEASPOON SALT

1 TEASPOON BAKING SODA

1 TEASPOON CREAM OF TARTAR

In a large mixing bowl, cream butter, brown sugar, and eggs. Stir in vanilla. Sift together dry ingredients and blend into creamed mixture. Shape into a 2-inch log. Wrap in waxed paper and chill overnight. To bake, slice log into ¼-inch-thick rounds. Place on an ungreased cookie sheet and bake at 350° for 10 to 12 minutes.
Yield: 4 dozen cookies

Candied Drop Cookies

2 CUPS FLOUR

2 TEASPOONS BAKING POWDER

½ TEASPOON SALT

½ CUP BUTTER, SOFTENED

2 CUPS BROWN SUGAR, PACKED

2 LARGE EGGS

2 TABLESPOONS HEAVY CREAM

2 CUPS CHOPPED PECANS

1 CUP GOLDEN RAISINS, CHOPPED

1 CUP CANDIED CHERRIES, CHOPPED

In a small bowl, combine flour, baking powder, and salt. Set aside. In a large bowl, cream butter and brown sugar. Beat in eggs and cream. Gradually add dry ingredients. Stir until well blended. Fold in pecans, raisins, and cherries. Drop by teaspoonfuls 1½ inches apart on lightly greased cookie sheets. Bake at 325° for 15 to 20 minutes, until cookies begin to color lightly. Transfer to cooling racks to cool completely.
Yield: 3 to 4 dozen cookies

A small ice cream scoop makes wonderfully uniform-sized drop cookies.

Candy Bar Cookies

1 CUP BUTTER OR MARGARINE, SOFTENED

1 CUP CREAMY PEANUT BUTTER

1 CUP SUGAR

1 CUP BROWN SUGAR, PACKED

2 LARGE EGGS, LIGHTLY BEATEN

2 TEASPOONS VANILLA EXTRACT

3 CUPS FLOUR

1 TEASPOON BAKING POWDER

1 TEASPOON BAKING SODA

1 (16 OUNCE) MILK CHOCOLATE CANDY BAR, CHOPPED INTO ½-INCH SQUARES

GLAZE:

1 CUP POWDERED SUGAR

2 TABLESPOONS COCOA

1 TABLESPOON MILK

In a large bowl, beat together butter, peanut butter, sugar, and brown sugar until light and fluffy. Add eggs and vanilla and beat well. In another bowl, combine flour, baking powder, and baking soda. Stir into creamed mixture. Form a teaspoonful of dough around each piece of chopped chocolate and bake at 350° on ungreased cookie sheets for 10 to 12 minutes. Cool completely.

For chocolate glaze, combine powdered sugar, cocoa, and milk until smooth. Add additional milk slowly to reach desired drizzling consistency. Drizzle cooled cookies with glaze.

Yield: 5 dozen cookies

Candy Cane Cookies

2½ CUPS FLOUR

1 TEASPOON SALT

1 CUP BUTTER, SOFTENED

1 CUP POWDERED SUGAR

1 EGG

1 TEASPOON PEPPERMINT EXTRACT

1 TEASPOON VANILLA EXTRACT

½ TEASPOON RED FOOD COLORING

In a small bowl, combine flour and salt. Set aside. In a large mixing bowl, cream butter and powdered sugar until fluffy. Add egg, peppermint extract, and vanilla; beat until smooth. Gradually add in dry ingredients and stir until thoroughly incorporated. Divide dough in half. Mix red food coloring into one-half of dough, stirring until coloring is even. For each cookie, shape about 2 teaspoons of plain dough into a 4-inch rope by rolling it back and forth on a lightly floured surface. Repeat with colored dough. Place plain rope and red rope side-by-side, pressing them together lightly; then twist together. Place cookies on greased cookie sheets and curve one end to form a candy cane shape. Bake at 350° for 8 to 10 minutes or until set. Yield: 2 dozen cookies

Give the gift of tasty treats from your kitchen this Christmas. After all, who can resist a gift baked with love? Wrap a stack of cookies with colored plastic wrap and secure with festive ribbon.

Chocolate-Filled Pinwheels

2 CUPS FLOUR

1 TEASPOON BAKING POWDER

½ TEASPOON SALT

¾ CUP VEGETABLE SHORTENING

1 CUP SUGAR

1 LARGE EGG

1 TABLESPOON VANILLA EXTRACT

FILLING:

1 CUP (6 OUNCES) SEMISWEET CHOCOLATE CHIPS

2 TABLESPOONS BUTTER

1 CUP FINELY GROUND WALNUTS

½ TABLESPOON VANILLA EXTRACT

Combine flour, baking powder, and salt. Set aside. Cream shortening and sugar. Beat in egg and vanilla. Gradually blend in dry ingredients. Remove ⅔ cup dough and set aside. Cover and chill remaining dough for 2 hours.

To prepare filling, melt chocolate chips and butter in double boiler over low heat, stirring constantly until smooth. Remove from heat and stir in vanilla. Blend in reserved dough. To assemble cookies, roll out chilled dough into a 12 x 16-inch rectangle on a lightly floured surface. Spread chocolate mixture over dough to within ¼ inch of edges. Beginning on long side, roll up dough jelly-roll fashion. Pinch seam to seal. Cut roll in half to create two 8-inch logs. Wrap well in waxed paper and chill for 8 hours or overnight.

To bake, heat oven to 350°. Slice logs into ¼-inch-thick slices and place 2 inches apart on ungreased cookie sheets. Bake for 10 to 12 minutes, until lightly golden. Cool on wire racks.

Yield: 4 to 5 dozen cookies

Chocolate Marshmallow Bars

¾ CUP BUTTER OR MARGARINE, SOFTENED

1½ CUPS SUGAR

3 EGGS

1 TEASPOON VANILLA EXTRACT

1⅓ CUPS FLOUR

½ TEASPOON BAKING POWDER

½ TEASPOON SALT

3 TABLESPOONS COCOA

4 CUPS MINIATURE MARSHMALLOWS

TOPPING:

1⅓ CUPS (8 OUNCES) MILK CHOCOLATE CHIPS

1 CUP CRUNCHY PEANUT BUTTER

3 TABLESPOONS BUTTER OR MARGARINE

2 CUPS CRISP RICE CEREAL

In a large mixing bowl, cream butter and sugar. Add eggs and vanilla; beat until fluffy. Combine flour, baking powder, salt, and cocoa; gradually add to creamed mixture. Spread in a greased jelly roll pan. Bake at 350° for 15 to 18 minutes. Sprinkle marshmallows evenly over cake; return to oven for 2 to 3 minutes. Dip knife or spatula in water and spread melted marshmallows evenly over cake. Cool completely.

For topping, combine chocolate chips, peanut butter, and butter in a medium saucepan. Cook over low heat, stirring constantly, until melted and well blended. Remove from heat and stir in cereal. Spread evenly over bars. Chill.

Yield: 3 dozen bars

Coconut Butterballs

1 CUP BUTTER, SOFTENED (NO SUBSTITUTIONS)

½ CUP POWDERED SUGAR

2 CUPS FLOUR

1½ CUPS SWEETENED, FLAKED COCONUT, COARSELY CHOPPED

POWDERED SUGAR

In a large bowl, cream butter and ½ cup powdered sugar. Gradually blend in flour. Fold in coconut. Roll dough into 1-inch balls. Roll in powdered sugar and place 1 inch apart on ungreased cookie sheets. Bake at 350° for 18 to 20 minutes, until lightly colored. Roll in powdered sugar again and cool on wire racks.
Yield: 4 dozen cookies

*In winter, use a table on your porch as a place
to quickly cool cookies and candies.*

Coconut Macaroons

3 LARGE EGG WHITES

⅛ TEASPOON SALT

⅛ TEASPOON CREAM OF TARTAR

¾ CUP SUGAR

1 TEASPOON VANILLA EXTRACT

1¼ CUPS SWEETENED, FLAKED COCONUT

1 TABLESPOON CORNSTARCH

Lightly grease 2 cookie sheets. Combine egg whites, salt, and cream of tartar in a bowl; beat until soft peaks form. Beat in sugar one tablespoon at a time until egg whites are stiff and shiny. Fold in vanilla. Toss coconut with cornstarch and fold mixture into the egg whites. Drop by teaspoonfuls onto baking sheets. Bake at 325° for 20 minutes, until edges are browned. Cool completely on wire racks.
Yield: 3 dozen cookies

Cranberry-Pecan Bars

1 CUP FLOUR

2 TABLESPOONS SUGAR

⅓ CUP BUTTER OR MARGARINE, SOFTENED

1 CUP FINELY CHOPPED PECANS, DIVIDED

1¼ CUPS SUGAR

2 TABLESPOONS ALL-PURPOSE FLOUR

2 EGGS, BEATEN

2 TABLESPOONS MILK

1 TABLESPOON FINELY GRATED ORANGE PEEL

1 TEASPOON VANILLA EXTRACT

1 CUP CHOPPED CRANBERRIES

½ CUP SWEETENED, FLAKED COCONUT

In a medium mixing bowl, combine 1 cup flour and 2 tablespoons sugar. With a pastry blender, cut butter into flour mixture until mixture resembles coarse crumbs. Stir in ½ cup pecans. Press flour mixture into the bottom of an ungreased 9 x 13-inch baking pan. Bake at 350° for 15 minutes. Meanwhile, combine 1¼ cups sugar and 2 tablespoons flour. Add eggs, milk, orange peel, and vanilla. Fold in cranberries, coconut, and remaining chopped pecans. Spread over partially baked crust. Bake for 25 to 30 minutes, until top is golden. Cool completely in pan on a wire rack. Cut into bars while warm.
Yield: 3 dozen bars

Cream Cheese Walnut Kiffels

1 POUND BUTTER, NO SUBSTITUTES

1 (8 OUNCE) AND 1 (3 OUNCE) PACKAGE CREAM CHEESE, SOFTENED

3 EGG YOLKS

4 CUPS FLOUR

WALNUT FILLING:

3 EGG WHITES

½ CUP SUGAR

1 POUND GROUND WALNUTS

½ TEASPOON VANILLA EXTRACT

In a mixing bowl, cream butter and cream cheese. Add egg yolks and mix well. Stir in flour and combine thoroughly. Divide dough into four sections. Wrap in plastic wrap and refrigerate overnight.

The next day, beat egg whites until soft peaks form. Add sugar and beat until stiff. Fold in walnuts and vanilla. Set aside.

Roll each section of dough into a circle about ¼ inch thick. Using a pizza cutter, divide circle into eight triangles. Place 1 to 1½ teaspoons of filling at the widest end of each section. Fold top two corners of triangle inward to touch and seal in the filling. Roll the top down toward the narrow point of the triangle. Place cookies on ungreased cookie sheets and bake at 350° for 13 to 15 minutes, until kiffels are golden. Remove from cookie sheets while still warm.

Yield: 3 dozen cookies

Crescent Cookies

¾ CUP BUTTER, COLD
(NO SUBSTITUTIONS)

2 CUPS FLOUR

3 TABLESPOONS SUGAR

1 CUP CHOPPED PECANS

½ TEASPOON SALT

3 TABLESPOONS ICE WATER

1 TEASPOON VANILLA EXTRACT

2 CUPS POWDERED SUGAR

Cut butter into flour until mixture resembles fine crumbs. Add sugar, pecans, and salt. Mix well, adding enough ice water to make a stiff dough. Add vanilla extract and knead lightly. Roll out on floured board to ¼-inch thickness. Cut into crescent shapes using a small glass coated with flour. Bake at 350° until bottoms are lightly browned. While cookies are hot, coat in powdered sugar.
Yield: 4 dozen crescents

Bake up oodles of Christmas cookies and hand-deliver them to your neighbors. Attach signature gift tags. You can find several free gift tag designs online, print your own tags on holiday labels, or create your own using card stock, colored pens, stamps, and stickers.

Let us remember that the Christmas heart is a giving heart, a wide-open heart that thinks of others first. The birth of the baby Jesus stands as the most significant event in all history, because it has meant the pouring into a sick world of the healing medicine of love which has transformed all manner of hearts for almost two thousand years. Underneath all the bulging bundles is this beating Christmas heart.
GEORGE MATTHEW ADAMS

Crunchy Christmas Cookies

1 CUP FLOUR

½ TEASPOON BAKING SODA

¼ TEASPOON BAKING POWDER

¼ TEASPOON SALT

½ CUP BUTTER OR MARGARINE, SOFTENED

½ CUP BROWN SUGAR, PACKED

1 LARGE EGG, LIGHTLY BEATEN

1 TEASPOON VANILLA EXTRACT

1 CUP OLD-FASHIONED OATS

1 CUP CORNFLAKES

½ CUP SWEETENED, FLAKED COCONUT

½ CUP COARSELY CHOPPED PECANS

In a small bowl, combine flour, baking soda, baking powder, and salt; set aside. In a large mixing bowl, cream butter and brown sugar until light and fluffy. Add egg and vanilla and beat well. Stir in flour mixture just until mixed. Stir in oats, cornflakes, coconut, and pecans.

Shape dough into 1-inch balls; place 2 inches apart on lightly greased cookie sheets. Bake at 350° for 10 to 12 minutes. Transfer to wire racks to cool completely.

Yield: 3 dozen cookies

Gingersnaps

2 CUPS FLOUR

2 TEASPOONS BAKING SODA

¼ TEASPOON SALT

1 TEASPOON GROUND CINNAMON

1 TEASPOON GROUND CLOVES

1 TEASPOON GROUND GINGER

¾ CUP BUTTER OR MARGARINE

1 CUP SUGAR

1 EGG

¼ CUP MOLASSES

ADDITIONAL SUGAR

In a small bowl, sift together flour, baking soda, salt, cinnamon, cloves, and ginger. Set aside. In a mixing bowl, cream together butter and sugar. Add the egg and molasses and beat well. Gradually mix in dry ingredients. Mix well. Chill dough. Form dough into 1-inch balls and roll in additional sugar. Place balls 2 inches apart on ungreased cookie sheets. Bake at 375° for 10 minutes or until cookies are set and tops are beginning to crack. Cool on wire racks.
Yield: 4 dozen cookies

Lebkuchen
(German Christmas Cookies)

¾ CUP HONEY

¾ CUP DARK BROWN SUGAR, PACKED

2 TABLESPOONS BUTTER

3 TO 4 TABLESPOONS WATER

1 LARGE EGG

GRATED PEEL OF 1 ORANGE

3½ CUPS FLOUR

½ TEASPOON BAKING SODA

½ TEASPOON SALT

1 TEASPOON CINNAMON

1 TEASPOON ALLSPICE

½ TEASPOON GROUND NUTMEG

½ TEASPOON GROUND GINGER

½ CUP FINELY CHOPPED MIXED CANDIED FRUIT

¾ CUP SLIVERED ALMONDS, FINELY CHOPPED

GLAZE:
1 CUP POWDERED SUGAR
3 TABLESPOONS WATER

Pour honey into a medium saucepan. Add dark brown sugar and butter and stir over moderate heat until sugar dissolves and butter melts. Do not boil. Remove from heat and cool to room temperature. Stir in egg and orange peel. Sift together flour, baking soda, salt, and spices; fold into honey mixture. Stir in candied fruit and almonds. Chill overnight.

Heat oven to 350°. Divide dough into four sections. Roll each portion on a lightly floured surface into a 5 x 6-inch rectangle, ¾ inch thick. Cut the dough into 1 x 2½-inch bars. Place bars on lightly greased cookie sheets. Bake for 10 minutes; transfer bars to wire cooling racks. Cool completely.

To make glaze, combine powdered sugar with 3 tablespoons water; blend well. Add additional water if glaze is too thick. Spread a thin coat on each cooled cookie.

Yield: 5 dozen cookies

Lemon Wafers

½ CUP BUTTER, SOFTENED

½ CUP SUGAR

2 LARGE EGGS, LIGHTLY BEATEN

1 TEASPOON VANILLA EXTRACT

GRATED PEEL OF 2 LEMONS

1 TEASPOON LEMON JUICE

1¼ CUPS SIFTED FLOUR

⅛ TEASPOON SALT

Cream butter and sugar in a large bowl until light and fluffy. Add eggs, vanilla, lemon peel, and juice; mix well. Fold in flour and salt. Chill for at least 1 hour. Heat oven to 350°. Lightly grease cookie sheets. Drop dough by teaspoonfuls about 1½ inches apart onto prepared cookie sheets. Bake for 6 to 7 minutes, until edges are very lightly browned. Cool on pans for 2 to 3 minutes. Transfer to wire racks to cool completely.
Yield: 4 dozen cookies

An old shirt makes a quick apron for your little helper. Use the arms to tie the shirt around your child's waist.

Meringue Kisses

2 EGG WHITES

⅛ TEASPOON SALT

⅔ CUP POWDERED SUGAR

⅔ CUP SEMISWEET CHOCOLATE CHIPS

⅓ CUP CHOPPED PECANS

In a mixing bowl, beat egg whites until foamy. Add salt, then gradually add sugar, one tablespoon a time, beating until very stiff peaks form. Fold in chocolate chips and pecans. Drop by teaspoonfuls onto lightly greased cookie sheets. Put in a 350° oven and turn off heat. Leave overnight. These are best served the same day.
Yield: 2 dozen cookies

No-Bake Date Balls

1 CUP CHOPPED DATES

1 CUP SUGAR

3 TABLESPOONS BUTTER

1 EGG, BEATEN

1 TEASPOON VANILLA EXTRACT

2 CUPS CRISP RICE CEREAL

¾ CUP CHOPPED PECANS

1 CUP SWEETENED, FLAKED COCONUT, CHOPPED

Combine dates, sugar, butter, and egg in a heavy saucepan. Cook over low heat, stirring constantly, until dates are softened and mixture is thickened and bubbly. Remove from heat and cool slightly. Mix in vanilla, rice cereal, and pecans. When mixture is cool enough to handle, form into 1-inch balls and roll in chopped coconut.
Yield: 2 dozen balls

Peanut Butter Kiss Cookies

1¾ CUPS FLOUR

1 TEASPOON BAKING POWDER

¾ TEASPOON BAKING SODA

¼ TEASPOON SALT

½ CUP BUTTER OR MARGARINE

½ CUP CREAMY PEANUT BUTTER

½ CUP SUGAR

½ CUP BROWN SUGAR, PACKED

1 EGG

1 TEASPOON VANILLA EXTRACT

ADDITIONAL SUGAR

48 CHOCOLATE KISSES

In a small bowl, mix first four ingredients. Set aside. In a mixing bowl, cream butter, peanut butter, and sugars. Add egg and vanilla; blend well. Stir in flour mixture. Form dough into 1-inch balls and roll in sugar. Place balls on greased cookie sheets. Bake at 375° for 10 minutes or until just golden brown. Place unwrapped chocolate kiss in center of each cookie while cookies are still warm.

Yield: 4 dozen cookies

Uplift the spirits of your friends and coworkers with this inexpensive Christmas gift idea: Pick out an assortment of holiday-shaped cookie cutters—stars, snowmen, Christmas trees, wreaths—and use red and green ribbon to attach a great recipe for cutout cookies.

Pecan Pie Bars

2 CUPS FLOUR

1 CUP BROWN SUGAR, PACKED

1 CUP BUTTER

5 EGGS, BEATEN

1 CUP DARK CORN SYRUP

¾ CUP SUGAR

1 PINCH SALT

1½ TEASPOONS VANILLA EXTRACT

1 CUP BROKEN PECANS

In a large bowl, blend flour and brown sugar. Cut in butter with pastry blender until mixture resembles coarse crumbs. Press crumb mixture into a well-greased 9 x 13-inch baking pan. Bake at 350° for 10 minutes or until golden. Meanwhile, combine eggs, corn syrup, sugar, salt, and vanilla. Blend well. Stir in pecans. Pour filling over hot crust. Reduce oven temperature to 275° and bake for 50 minutes or until center is set. Cool in pan on a wire rack before cutting into bars.
Yield: 3 dozen bars

Scottish Shortbread

1 CUP BUTTER, SOFTENED (NO SUBSTITUTIONS)

½ CUP PLUS 2 TABLESPOONS SUGAR, DIVIDED

2 CUPS SIFTED FLOUR

¼ TEASPOON SALT

¼ TEASPOON BAKING POWDER

Beat butter until light and creamy. Add ½ cup sugar and beat until mixture is fluffy. Sift flour with salt and baking powder; stir into butter mixture. Place dough on an ungreased baking sheet and pat into a ½-inch-thick rectangle. Score dough into 1 x 2-inch bars with the point of a knife. Sprinkle with remaining sugar and bake in the center of the oven at 350° for 15 minutes, until edges are lightly browned. Cool shortbread on the baking sheet for 15 minutes; cut into bars as marked.
Yield: 2 dozen bars

Sesame Seed Cookies

1 CUP SESAME SEEDS

½ CUP SWEETENED, FLAKED COCONUT

½ CUP BUTTER, SOFTENED

1 CUP BROWN SUGAR, PACKED

1 LARGE EGG

2 TEASPOONS VANILLA EXTRACT

GRATED PEEL OF 1 LEMON

2 CUPS FLOUR

1 TEASPOON BAKING POWDER

½ TEASPOON BAKING SODA

⅛ TEASPOON SALT

Toast sesame seeds and coconut in the oven on an ungreased cookie sheet at 350° for 7 to 8 minutes, stirring 2 to 3 times. Remove from oven; stir and set aside.

Cream butter and sugar until light and fluffy. Stir in egg, vanilla, lemon peel, and cooled sesame seeds and coconut. Sift together flour, baking powder, baking soda, and salt. Fold into butter mixture. Shape dough into ½-inch balls. Place on lightly greased cookie sheets and bake for 10 minutes or until lightly browned. Cool completely on wire racks.
Yield: 3 dozen cookies

Sour Cream Walnut Cookies

½ CUP BUTTER, SOFTENED

¼ CUP SUGAR

1 LARGE EGG YOLK

½ CUP SOUR CREAM

1½ CUPS SIFTED FLOUR

½ TEASPOON BAKING SODA

½ TEASPOON GROUND CLOVES

½ CUP GROUND WALNUTS

GRATED PEEL OF 1 ORANGE

Cream butter and sugar in a large bowl until light and fluffy. Blend in egg yolk and sour cream. Sift flour with baking soda and cloves; fold into butter mixture. Stir in walnuts and orange peel. Shape dough into a ball and chill for at least 1 hour.

Grease cookie sheets. Form chilled dough into 1-inch balls. Place balls on cookie sheets and flatten gently with a fork. Bake at 325° for 10 minutes or until edges are lightly browned. Transfer cookies to wire racks to cool. Yield: 2 dozen cookies

Velvet Sugar Cookies

2 CUPS BUTTER, SOFTENED

1 (8 OUNCE) PACKAGE CREAM
CHEESE, SOFTENED

2 CUPS SUGAR

2 EGG YOLKS

2 TEASPOONS VANILLA EXTRACT

4½ CUPS FLOUR

¼ TEASPOON SALT

In a large mixing bowl, cream together butter, cream cheese, and sugar until light and fluffy. Add in egg yolks and vanilla; mix well. Gradually stir in flour and salt. Chill for 2 hours. Roll out dough on a floured surface and cut into desired shapes. Place on greased baking sheets and bake at 350° for 9 to 12 minutes. Cool on cookie sheets before transferring to wire racks. Frost if desired.

FROSTING:

4 TABLESPOONS BUTTER,
SOFTENED

1 (3 OUNCE) PACKAGE CREAM
CHEESE, SOFTENED

3 CUPS POWDERED SUGAR,
DIVIDED

3 TABLESPOONS MILK

½ TEASPOON VANILLA EXTRACT

Food coloring (optional)

In a mixing bowl, beat together butter, cream cheese, and 1 cup powdered sugar until smooth. Add in milk and vanilla. Gradually mix in remaining powdered sugar and beat until smooth and of a spreadable consistency. Divide frosting and tint with food coloring if desired.
Yield: 3 dozen cookies

Wilma's Thumbprint Cookies

½ CUP SHORTENING

¼ CUP BROWN SUGAR, PACKED

1 EGG YOLK

½ TEASPOON VANILLA

1 CUP FLOUR

¼ TEASPOON SALT

1 EGG WHITE, SLIGHTLY BEATEN

¾ CUP FINELY CHOPPED NUTS

Thoroughly mix shortening, sugar, egg yolk, and vanilla. Sift flour and salt; then stir into shortening mixture and blend. Roll into 1-inch balls; dip into egg white and roll in nuts. Place 1 inch apart on ungreased cookie sheets. Make a thumbprint in the center of each cookie. Bake at 350° for 8 to 10 minutes. Do not let cookies get too brown.

ICING:

1 POUND POWDERED SUGAR

¼ TEASPOON SALT

4 TABLESPOONS MILK

1 TEASPOON VANILLA

6 TABLESPOONS SOFT BUTTER

Blend all ingredients until smooth. Fill thumbprints with icing.
Yield: 2 dozen cookies

When you want to freeze cookies that have been frosted, place them in a single layer on a baking sheet in the freezer for 2 hours. When frozen, they can be stacked or bagged in a freezer container. When ready to use, be sure to seperate the cookies in a single layer on a serving tray before they begin to thaw.

CAKES

Banana Nut Cake

2½ CUPS FLOUR

1⅔ CUPS SUGAR

1¼ TEASPOONS BAKING SODA

1¼ TEASPOONS BAKING POWDER

1 TEASPOON SALT

⅔ CUP SHORTENING

1¼ CUPS MASHED BANANAS

⅓ CUP BUTTERMILK

2 EGGS, LIGHTLY BEATEN

1 CUP CHOPPED WALNUTS

FROSTING:

1 (1 POUND) BOX POWDERED SUGAR

½ CUP BUTTER, SOFTENED

⅛ TEASPOON SALT

1 TEASPOON VANILLA EXTRACT

2 TABLESPOONS MILK

½ BANANA, MASHED

Combine dry ingredients. Add shortening and mashed bananas and mix with large spoon for 2 minutes. Add buttermilk and eggs; blend well. Fold in walnuts. Pour batter in a 9 x 13-inch greased and floured pan. Bake at 350° for 40 minutes or until cake tests done with a toothpick. Cool completely.

For frosting, cream together powdered sugar, butter, and salt. Blend in vanilla, milk, and mashed banana. Beat until creamy. Spread on cooled cake. Yield: 15 servings

Banana Pudding Cake

2 SMALL RIPE BANANAS, MASHED

1 PACKAGE YELLOW CAKE MIX

1 (4 SERVING SIZE) PACKAGE INSTANT VANILLA PUDDING

4 EGGS, LIGHTLY BEATEN

1 CUP WATER

¼ CUP VEGETABLE OIL

½ CUP FINELY CHOPPED NUTS (OPTIONAL)

WHIPPED TOPPING (OPTIONAL)

Mash bananas in a mixing bowl. Add cake mix, pudding mix, eggs, water, and vegetable oil. Beat at medium speed for 2 minutes. Fold in nuts. Pour into a greased and floured 9 x 13-inch cake pan and bake at 350° for 50 to 55 minutes. Top with whipped topping if desired.
Yield: 12 to 15 servings

Martha and I love Christmas traditions! Why not start a new one with your family this year?

Best Carrot Cake

4 EGGS	3 TEASPOONS GROUND CINNAMON
1½ CUPS VEGETABLE OIL	1 TEASPOON SALT
2 CUPS SUGAR	3 CUPS SHREDDED CARROTS
2 TEASPOONS VANILLA EXTRACT	½ CUP CHOPPED WALNUTS
2 CUPS FLOUR	½ CUP GOLDEN RAISINS
2 TEASPOONS BAKING POWDER	½ CUP SWEETENED, FLAKED
2 TEASPOONS BAKING SODA	COCONUT

CREAM CHEESE FROSTING:

½ CUP BUTTER, SOFTENED	1 POUND POWDERED SUGAR
1 (8 OUNCE) PACKAGE CREAM CHEESE, SOFTENED	1 TO 2 TABLESPOONS MILK
1 TEASPOON VANILLA EXTRACT	

In a large mixing bowl, lightly beat eggs. Add oil. Stir in sugar and vanilla. In a separate bowl, combine flour, baking powder, baking soda, cinnamon, and salt. Gradually blend dry ingredients into egg mixture. Stir in shredded carrots, walnuts, raisins, and coconut. Divide batter evenly between three greased and floured 9-inch round baking pans. Bake at 350° for 20 to 25 minutes or until wooden pick inserted in center comes out clean. Allow cake to cool in pans for 10 minutes; then transfer from pans to wire racks to cool completely.

For frosting, beat butter with cream cheese. Add vanilla. Gradually beat in powdered sugar. Beat in enough milk to reach a fluffy frosting consistency. Frost cooled cake.

Yield: 12 to 16 servings

Butterscotch-Pumpkin Bundt Cake

1 (11 OUNCE) PACKAGE BUTTERSCOTCH CHIPS, DIVIDED

2 CUPS FLOUR

1¾ CUPS SUGAR

1 TABLESPOON BAKING POWDER

1½ TEASPOONS GROUND CINNAMON

1 TEASPOON SALT

½ TEASPOON GROUND NUTMEG

1 CUP PUMPKIN PUREE

½ CUP VEGETABLE OIL

3 LARGE EGGS

1 TEASPOON VANILLA EXTRACT

3 TABLESPOONS POWDERED SUGAR

Prepare 12-cup Bundt pan. Melt 1 cup butterscotch chips in small, microwave-safe bowl on medium power for 1 minute; stir. Microwave at additional 10-second intervals, stirring until chips are completely melted. Cool to room temperature. In a medium bowl, combine flour, sugar, baking powder, cinnamon, salt, and nutmeg. In a large mixing bowl, whisk together melted chips, pumpkin, vegetable oil, eggs, and vanilla. Stir in dry mixture. Blend in remaining chips. Pour batter into prepared Bundt pan. Bake at 350° for 40 to 50 minutes or until wooden pick inserted in cake comes out clean. Cool in pan on a wire rack for 30 minutes; remove from pan to cool completely. Sprinkle with powdered sugar.
Yield: 16 servings

Candy Cane Cheesecake

1⅓ CUPS CHOCOLATE COOKIE
CRUMBS

2 TABLESPOONS SUGAR

¼ CUP BUTTER

3 (8 OUNCE) PACKAGES CREAM
CHEESE, SOFTENED

2 TABLESPOONS BUTTER,
SOFTENED

1½ CUPS SOUR CREAM

½ CUP SUGAR

3 EGGS

1 TABLESPOON FLOUR

2 TEASPOONS VANILLA EXTRACT

¼ TEASPOON PEPPERMINT
EXTRACT

⅔ CUP CRUSHED PEPPERMINT
CANDIES

SWEETENED WHIPPED TOPPING
(OPTIONAL)

Combine cookie crumbs, sugar, and ¼ cup butter; press into a 9-inch springform pan. In a medium bowl, beat cream cheese and 2 tablespoons butter. Blend in sour cream, sugar, eggs, flour, vanilla, and peppermint extract until smooth. Stir in crushed candy. Pour into crust and bake on lowest rack of 325° oven for 50 to 60 minutes or until firm. Allow to cool completely; refrigerate overnight. When ready to serve, remove sides of pan. Top with sweetened whipped topping if desired.
Yield: 12 servings

Have a Christmas birthday celebration—celebrating the birth of Baby Jesus. Bake a cake and include the works—candles, ice cream, and balloons. Sing "Happy Birthday" to Jesus with your children.

Chocolate Cream Cheese Bundt Cake

1¼ CUPS SEMISWEET CHOCOLATE CHIPS

2 (8 OUNCE) PACKAGES CREAM CHEESE, SOFTENED

¾ CUP SUGAR

3 TABLESPOONS MILK

1 PACKAGE CHOCOLATE CAKE MIX

¾ CUP BREWED COFFEE, COOLED

¼ CUP VEGETABLE OIL

3 LARGE EGGS, LIGHTLY BEATEN

⅔ CUP CHOPPED NUTS

½ CUP HEAVY CREAM

Grease and flour a Bundt pan. Microwave chocolate chips on medium power for 1 minute; stir. Continue to heat at 10-second intervals until chocolate is melted completely. Cool to room temperature. In a medium mixing bowl, combine cream cheese, sugar, milk, and melted chocolate. Beat until smooth. Set aside. In another bowl, combine cake mix, coffee, vegetable oil, and eggs; beat for 4 minutes. Pour into prepared pan and sprinkle with nuts. Spoon cream cheese mixture over cake mix, but do not allow cream cheese mixture to touch sides of pan. Bake at 350° for 55 to 65 minutes, until top springs back when pressed lightly in center. Cool in pan for 1 hour before inverting.

GLAZE:

½ CUP HEAVY CREAM

½ CUP SEMISWEET CHOCOLATE CHIPS

For glaze, heat cream in a small saucepan over medium heat until cream just begins to boil. Remove from heat and stir in chocolate chips until melted and smooth. Drizzle warm glaze over cooled cake. Store, covered, in refrigerator.
Yield: 12 servings

Chocolate Sour Cream
Sheet Cake

1 CUP WATER

1 CUP BUTTER OR MARGARINE

¼ CUP COCOA

2 LARGE EGGS, LIGHTLY BEATEN

1 (8 OUNCE) CARTON SOUR CREAM

2 CUPS SUGAR

2 CUPS FLOUR

1 TEASPOON BAKING SODA

⅛ TEASPOON SALT

½ CUP SEMISWEET CHOCOLATE CHIPS

In a medium saucepan, combine water, butter, and cocoa. Bring to a boil and boil for two minutes. Set aside to cool slightly. In a mixing bowl, blend eggs, sour cream, sugar, flour, baking soda, and salt. Add cocoa mixture and blend well. Stir in chocolate chips. Spread batter into a greased and floured 10 x 15-inch jelly roll pan. Bake at 375° for 20 to 25 minutes. Cool slightly before icing.

ICING:

6 TABLESPOONS MILK

6 TABLESPOONS COCOA

1 CUP BUTTER OR MARGARINE

1 POUND POWDERED SUGAR

1½ TEASPOONS VANILLA EXTRACT

In a saucepan, boil milk, cocoa, and butter for three minutes. Remove from heat. Beat in powdered sugar and vanilla until icing is smooth and glossy. Pour over warm cake and spread evenly.
Yield: 24 servings

Classic Cherry Cheesecake

1½ CUPS GRAHAM CRACKER CRUMBS

2 TABLESPOONS SUGAR

¼ CUP PLUS 2 TABLESPOONS BUTTER OR MARGARINE, MELTED

1 TEASPOON GRATED LEMON PEEL

3 (8 OUNCE) PACKAGES CREAM CHEESE, SOFTENED

1 CUP SUGAR

3 EGGS

½ TEASPOON VANILLA EXTRACT

1 (16 OUNCE) CARTON SOUR CREAM

3 TABLESPOONS SUGAR

½ TEASPOON VANILLA EXTRACT

1 (21 OUNCE) CAN CHERRY PIE FILLING

In a medium mixing bowl, combine graham cracker crumbs, 2 tablespoons sugar, butter, and lemon peel. Blend well. Press mixture firmly in bottom and up sides of a 9-inch springform pan. Bake at 350° for 5 minutes; set aside.

Increase oven temperature to 375°. In a large mixing bowl, beat cream cheese until light and fluffy; gradually add 1 cup sugar and beat well. Add eggs, one at a time, beating well after each addition. Stir in ½ teaspoon vanilla. Pour cream cheese mixture into prepared crust. Bake for 30 to 35 minutes or until cheesecake is set.

Increase oven temperature to 475°. Beat sour cream at medium speed for 2 minutes. Add 3 tablespoons sugar and ½ teaspoon vanilla; beat 1 additional minute. Carefully spread sour cream mixture evenly over cheesecake. Place cheesecake in oven for 5 to 7 minutes or until sour cream mixture is bubbly. Remove cheesecake from oven and place on a wire rack. Let cool in pan to room temperature. Top with cherry pie filling. Chill at least 8 hours. To serve, carefully remove sides of springform pan.
Yield: 10 to 12 servings

Cranberry Bundt Cake

2 CUPS FLOUR

1 TEASPOON BAKING POWDER

¾ TEASPOON BAKING SODA

½ TEASPOON SALT

⅔ CUP BUTTER OR MARGARINE, SOFTENED

1 CUP SUGAR

3 EGGS

1½ TEASPOONS VANILLA EXTRACT

1 (8 OUNCE) CARTON SOUR CREAM

¾ CUP CHOPPED DRIED CRANBERRIES

⅓ CUP CHOPPED PECANS

POWDERED SUGAR

In a small bowl, combine flour, baking powder, baking soda, and salt. Set aside. In a mixing bowl, cream butter with sugar. Add eggs one at a time, beating well after each addition. Stir in vanilla. Add dry ingredients to creamed mixture alternately with sour cream. Stir in cranberries and pecans and pour into greased and floured 8-inch Bundt cake pan. Bake at 350° for 45 to 50 minutes or until a wooden pick inserted in cake comes out clean. Cool for 10 minutes before removing from pan. Dust with powdered sugar. Yield: 8 to 10 servings

Cream Cheese Pound Cake

¾ CUP BUTTER (NO SUBSTITUTIONS)

1 (8 OUNCE) PACKAGE CREAM CHEESE, SOFTENED

½ CUP SUGAR

1½ TEASPOONS VANILLA EXTRACT

4 LARGE EGGS, LIGHTLY BEATEN

2 CUPS FLOUR

1½ TEASPOONS BAKING POWDER

¼ CUP POWDERED SUGAR

Grease and flour a loaf pan and set aside. Cream together butter, cream cheese, sugar, and vanilla. Add eggs one at a time, beating well after each addition. Sift together flour and baking powder; gradually add to creamed mixture. Pour into prepared pan. Bake at 325° for 1 hour or until wooden pick comes out clean. Let cake cool in pan for 5 minutes; remove from pan and sprinkle with powdered sugar.
Yield: 8 servings

Try to recapture the childlike wonder of the season by enjoying the simple pleasures. Build a snowman; have a friendly snowball fight with your kids; go ice skating or sled riding; read a book in front of a blazing fire; drive around town to view the holiday displays and lights; don't count calories when you're enjoying those holiday treats; and drink lots of hot chocolate!

Happy, happy Christmas, that can win us back to the delusions of our childhood days, recall to the old man the pleasures of his youth, and transport the traveler back to his own fireside and quiet home!

CHARLES DICKENS

Devil's Food Cake with Fluffy Frosting

2¼ CUPS FLOUR	¾ CUP VEGETABLE SHORTENING
⅔ CUP COCOA	1⅔ CUPS SUGAR
1¼ TEASPOONS BAKING SODA	2 LARGE EGGS
¼ TEASPOON BAKING POWDER	1 TEASPOON VANILLA EXTRACT
1 TEASPOON SALT	1½ CUPS WATER

Grease and flour a 9 x 13-inch baking pan. Combine flour, cocoa, baking soda, baking powder, and salt. Set aside. In a large mixing bowl, cream shortening and sugar. Beat in eggs and vanilla. Gradually add dry ingredients alternately with water. Beat on low speed for 30 seconds, then on high speed for 3 minutes, scraping bowl occasionally. Pour batter into prepared pan. Bake at 350° for 40 to 45 minutes or until a wooden pick inserted in center comes out clean. Cool on wire rack.

FROSTING:

¼ CUP FLOUR

1 CUP MILK

1 CUP BUTTER OR MARGARINE

1 CUP SUGAR

1 TEASPOON VANILLA EXTRACT

Whisk together flour and milk in a saucepan; cook until thick, stirring constantly. Remove from heat. Place lid on saucepan. Allow to cool, stirring frequently to keep mixture smooth. In a bowl, cream together butter, sugar, and vanilla; add flour and milk mixture. Beat until light and fluffy. Frost cooled cake.
Yield: 12 to 16 servings

Fruitcake

1 POUND PITTED DATES, CUT INTO PIECES

1 POUND GLAZED CHERRIES, HALVED

2 POUNDS CHOPPED PECANS

½ POUND SHREDDED COCONUT

1 POUND GLAZED PINEAPPLE, CUT INTO PIECES

1 (14 OUNCE) CAN SWEETENED CONDENSED MILK

2 TEASPOONS VANILLA EXTRACT

Grease three 8 x 4-inch loaf pans well. Mix dates, cherries, pecans, coconut, and pineapple in a large bowl. Add sweetened condensed milk and vanilla; blend well. Pack tightly in prepared pans. Bake at 275° for 1½ hours. Yield: 3 (2 pound) fruitcakes

Fill a canning jar with colorful candies. Tie a ribbon and tag around the neck of the jar, and you have an instant gift. Add a note tag that says, "You are a real sweetie" or "I appreciate your sweet friendship." You could also fill a jar with small cookie cutters and attach your favorite sugar cookie recipe.

Fruit and Nut Cake

1½ CUPS FLOUR

1½ CUPS SUGAR

1 TEASPOON BAKING POWDER

1 TEASPOON SALT

2 POUNDS WALNUTS, COARSELY CHOPPED

1 POUND BRAZIL NUTS, COARSELY CHOPPED

2 POUNDS PITTED DATES, COARSELY CHOPPED

1 (8 OUNCE) JAR MARASCHINO CHERRIES, DRAINED AND
COARSELY CHOPPED

5 EGGS, BEATEN

1 TEASPOON VANILLA EXTRACT

In a large mixing bowl, sift together flour, sugar, baking powder, and salt. Add in nuts, dates, and cherries. Stir well to coat. Combine eggs and vanilla; blend into flour mixture. Spoon into three well-greased loaf pans. Bake at 325° for 1 hour.
Yield: 24 servings

Fruit Cocktail Cake

2 CUPS FRUIT COCKTAIL

2 EGGS, WELL BEATEN

1½ CUPS SUGAR

2 CUPS FLOUR

2 TEASPOONS BAKING SODA

¼ TEASPOON SALT

½ CUP BROWN SUGAR, PACKED

½ CUP CHOPPED PECANS

ICING:

½ CUP BUTTER OR MARGARINE, SOFTENED

¾ CUP SUGAR

1 CUP SWEETENED, FLAKED COCONUT

½ CUP EVAPORATED MILK

1 TEASPOON VANILLA EXTRACT

In a mixing bowl, combine fruit cocktail, eggs, and sugar. Mix well. In a small bowl, combine flour, baking soda, and salt. Blend dry ingredients with fruit mixture. Pour into a buttered 9-inch square pan; sprinkle with brown sugar and pecans. Bake at 300° for 30 minutes or until cake tests done. Cool completely.

To prepare icing, cream butter with sugar. Add remaining ingredients and blend well. Frost cooled cake.

Yield: 9 to 12 servings

When you need to test the doneness of a cake or bread, and you don't have a cake-testing tool, use an uncooked piece of spaghetti. It is long enough to test the doneness of your deepest baked goods.

Grasshopper Cake

1 PACKAGE WHITE CAKE MIX

½ CUP CRÈME DE MENTHE, DIVIDED

1 (16 OUNCE) JAR FUDGE TOPPING

1 (12 OUNCE) CARTON WHIPPED TOPPING, THAWED

Prepare cake mix according to package directions. Stir in ¼ cup crème de menthe. Spread into a prepared 9 x 13-inch cake pan. Bake at 350° according to package directions, until cake tests done. Cool completely.

Spread cooled cake with fudge topping. Fold ¼ cup crème de menthe into thawed whipped topping. Spread evenly over fudge topping. Chill until ready to serve.

Yield: 12 to 16 servings

Start the New Year off right!
1. *Forgive and forget.*
2. *Set an attainable goal for the New Year.*
3. *Call an old friend to catch up.*
4. *Be thankful for what you have.*
5. *Make more time for family.*
6. *Vow to make a difference in the world.*
7. *Laugh.*
8. *Thank God every day for the Gift of Love He sent for you and me!*

Somehow, not only for Christmas, but all the long year through, the joy that you give to others is the joy that comes back to you.

JOHN GREENLEAF WHITTIER

Hummingbird Cake

3 CUPS FLOUR

2 CUPS SUGAR

1 TEASPOON SALT

1 TEASPOON BAKING SODA

1 TEASPOON GROUND CINNAMON

3 EGGS, BEATEN

1½ CUPS VEGETABLE OIL

2 TEASPOONS VANILLA EXTRACT

1 (8 OUNCE) CAN CRUSHED PINEAPPLE, UNDRAINED

2 CUPS CHOPPED BANANAS (ABOUT 4 MEDIUM)

2 CUPS CHOPPED PECANS, DIVIDED

Grease and flour three 9-inch round cake pans. In a large mixing bowl, combine dry ingredients. Add eggs and vegetable oil and stir until moistened. Stir in vanilla, pineapple, bananas, and 1 cup pecans. Divide batter evenly between cake pans. Bake at 350° for 25 minutes or until toothpick inserted in cake comes out clean. Cool for 10 minutes in pans, then transfer to wire cooling racks. Cool completely. Frost with cream cheese frosting and garnish with remaining pecans.

CREAM CHEESE FROSTING:

2 (8 OUNCE) PACKAGES CREAM CHEESE, SOFTENED

1 CUP BUTTER OR MARGARINE

1 (2 POUND) PACKAGE POWDERED SUGAR

2 TEASPOONS VANILLA EXTRACT

1 DASH SALT

Beat cream cheese and butter until smooth. Add powdered sugar and beat until light and fluffy. Beat in vanilla and salt. Spread between cooled cake layers and up sides and on top of cake. Garnish with chopped pecans. Yield: 8 to 12 servings

Italian Cream Cake

1 CUP BUTTER OR MARGARINE, SOFTENED	1 CUP MILK
2 CUPS SUGAR	⅔ CUP FINELY CHOPPED PECANS
5 EGGS, SEPARATED	1 (3½ OUNCE) CAN SWEETENED, FLAKED COCONUT
2½ CUPS FLOUR	2 TEASPOONS VANILLA EXTRACT
1 TEASPOON BAKING SODA	½ TEASPOON CREAM OF TARTAR

Grease and flour three 9-inch round cake pans. Line with waxed paper; grease paper. Cream butter; add sugar and beat well. Add egg yolks one at a time, beating after each addition. Combine flour and baking soda. Add to creamed mixture alternately with milk, beginning and ending with flour mixture. Stir in pecans, coconut, and vanilla. In a glass or metal mixing bowl, beat egg whites until foamy. Add cream of tartar; beat until stiff peaks form. Gently fold beaten egg whites into batter.

Pour batter into prepared pans. Bake at 350° for 25 to 30 minutes or until wooden pick inserted in cake comes out clean. Let cool in pans for 10 minutes. Remove from pans; peel off waxed paper and let cool completely on wire racks.

CREAM CHEESE FROSTING:

1 (8 OUNCE) PACKAGE CREAM CHEESE, SOFTENED

½ CUP BUTTER, SOFTENED

1 (16 OUNCE) PACKAGE POWDERED SUGAR, SIFTED

1 CUP CHOPPED PECANS

2 TEASPOONS VANILLA EXTRACT

Combine cream cheese and butter, beating until smooth. Gradually add powdered sugar and beat until light and fluffy. Stir in pecans and vanilla. Frost cooled cake.
Yield: 12 to 16 servings

Jewel Cakes

2 CUPS PECAN PIECES

1¾ CUPS WALNUT PIECES

1¼ CUPS GOLDEN RAISINS

½ POUND PITTED DATES, CHOPPED

¾ CUP RED CANDIED CHERRIES, COARSELY CHOPPED

¾ CUP GREEN CANDIED CHERRIES, COARSELY CHOPPED

1½ CUPS CANDIED PINEAPPLE, COARSELY CHOPPED

1 (14 OUNCE) CAN SWEETENED CONDENSED MILK

In a large mixing bowl, combine all ingredients and mix well with a large spoon. Pack tightly into well-greased mini muffin cups. Bake at 275° for 25 to 30 minutes.
Yield: 24 cakes

Lemon Pound Cake

1 (18¼ OUNCE) PACKAGE LEMON CAKE MIX

1 (4 SERVING SIZE) PACKAGE INSTANT LEMON PUDDING

4 LARGE EGGS

1 CUP WATER

⅓ CUP VEGETABLE OIL

POWDERED SUGAR

Grease and flour a 10-inch tube pan; set aside. In a large mixing bowl, combine cake mix, pudding mix, eggs, water, and vegetable oil. Beat at medium speed for 2 minutes. Pour into prepared pan. Bake at 350° for 50 to 60 minutes. Let cake cool in pan for 15 minutes on wire rack. Remove cake from pan and cool completely on wire rack. Sprinkle with powdered sugar. Yield: 12 servings

Oatmeal–Chocolate Chip Cake

1¾ CUPS BOILING WATER

1 CUP QUICK OR OLD-FASHIONED OATS

1 CUP BROWN SUGAR, PACKED

1 CUP SUGAR

3 TABLESPOONS MILK

½ CUP BUTTER OR MARGARINE

3 EGGS, BEATEN

1¾ CUPS FLOUR

1 TEASPOON BAKING SODA

½ TEASPOON SALT

2 TABLESPOONS COCOA

1 (12 OUNCE) PACKAGE MINI CHOCOLATE CHIPS, DIVIDED

1 CUP CHOPPED WALNUTS

Pour boiling water over oatmeal; let stand at room temperature for 15 minutes. Add sugars, milk, butter, and eggs; beat well. In a small bowl, combine flour, baking soda, salt, and cocoa. Gradually stir into oatmeal mixture. Stir in 1 cup chocolate chips. Pour into a greased 9 x 13-inch pan. Sprinkle remaining chocolate chips and walnuts on top. Bake at 350° for 40 minutes.
Yield: 12 servings

Old-Fashioned Gingerbread Cake

2 (10¾ OUNCE) CANS CONDENSED TOMATO SOUP

3 EGGS, LIGHTLY BEATEN

2 (14 OUNCE) PACKAGES GINGERBREAD MIX

1 CUP RAISINS

1 CUP CHOPPED WALNUTS

POWDERED SUGAR

In a large mixing bowl, blend soup and eggs. Stir in gingerbread mix. Blend at low speed until thoroughly moistened; beat 2 minutes on medium speed. Fold in raisins and nuts. Pour into a well-greased 9-inch tube pan. Bake at 325° for 1 hour and 15 minutes or until cake tests done. Cool in pan for 10 minutes; remove from pan. Sprinkle top with powdered sugar. Serve warm or at room temperature.
Yield: 12 servings

Father, Thank You for meeting all of my needs this year. I know I focus (too often) on the things I want rather than what I need. When I have a bad case of the "gimmes," please turn my thoughts toward thanks for the many blessings I do have. Touch the lives and hearts of those less fortunate than I, even in some small way. Give them hope—hope made possible only by You. Amen.

I will tell of the kindnesses of the LORD, the deeds for which he is to be praised, according to all the LORD has done for us— yes, the many good things he has done.
ISAIAH 63:7

Pineapple Upside-Down Cake

½ CUP BUTTER OR MARGARINE

1 CUP BROWN SUGAR, PACKED

3 (8¼ OUNCE) CANS PINEAPPLE
RINGS, UNDRAINED

10 PECAN HALVES

11 MARASCHINO CHERRIES,
HALVED

2 EGGS, SEPARATED

1 EGG YOLK

1 CUP SUGAR

1 CUP FLOUR

1 TEASPOON BAKING POWDER

½ TEASPOON GROUND CINNAMON

¼ TEASPOON SALT

1 TEASPOON VANILLA EXTRACT

¼ TEASPOON CREAM OF TARTAR

Melt butter in a 10-inch cast-iron skillet over low heat. Sprinkle brown sugar in skillet and remove from heat. Drain pineapple, reserving ¼ cup juice. Set juice aside. Cut pineapple rings in half, reserving 1 whole ring. Place whole pineapple ring in center of skillet. Arrange 10 pineapple pieces in a spoke fashion around whole ring in center of skillet. Place a pecan half and a maraschino cherry half between each piece of pineapple. Place a cherry half in center of whole pineapple ring. Arrange remaining pineapple pieces, cut side up, around sides of skillet. Place a cherry half in center of each piece of pineapple around sides of skillet.

Beat 3 egg yolks until thick and lemon colored. Gradually add 1 cup sugar, beating well. Combine flour, baking powder, cinnamon, and salt; stir well. Add to egg mixture alternately with reserved pineapple juice. Stir in vanilla. Beat egg whites and cream of tartar at high speed until stiff peaks form; fold beaten egg whites into batter. Spoon batter evenly over pineapple in skillet. Bake at 350° for 45 to 50 minutes or until cake is set. Invert cake onto a serving plate immediately. Cut into wedges to serve.
Yield: 8 servings

Toffee Coffee Cake

2 CUPS BROWN SUGAR, PACKED

2 CUPS FLOUR, SIFTED

1 CUP BUTTER OR MARGARINE

1 LARGE EGG, BEATEN

1 CUP BUTTERMILK

1 TEASPOON VANILLA EXTRACT

1 TEASPOON BAKING SODA

⅛ TEASPOON SALT

8 OUNCES TOFFEE CANDY, CRUSHED

½ CUP CHOPPED PECANS

In a medium bowl, combine brown sugar, flour, and butter to form a crumbly mixture. Reserve 1 cup for topping. In another bowl, combine egg, buttermilk, vanilla, baking soda, and salt. Add to first mixture; blend well with an electric mixer. Spoon into a greased 9 x 13-inch cake pan. Sprinkle with reserved topping, crushed toffee candy, and chopped pecans. Bake at 350° for 50 to 55 minutes.
Yield: 16 servings

Keep brown sugar soft by placing 2 to 3 large marshmallows in the canister with the brown sugar.

Tres Leches

1½ CUPS SUGAR	1½ TEASPOONS BAKING POWDER
¾ CUP BUTTER, SOFTENED	1 CUP MILK
9 EGGS, SEPARATED, ROOM TEMPERATURE	1 TEASPOON VANILLA EXTRACT
	1 TEASPOON CREAM OF TARTAR
2 CUPS FLOUR	

In a large mixing bowl, cream sugar and butter together until light and fluffy. Add egg yolks and beat until fluffy again, 2 to 3 minutes on medium-high speed. In a small bowl, combine flour and baking powder. In a third bowl, mix milk and vanilla. Alternately add flour mixture and milk mixture to butter mixture until all are combined.

Beat egg whites with cream of tartar until soft peaks form; gently fold into flour and butter mixture. Pour batter into a greased 9 x 13-inch cake pan; bake at 350° for approximately 25 minutes, until golden brown. Poke holes in cake with fork or wooden skewer. Cool.

THREE MILKS:

2 CUPS HEAVY CREAM

1 (5 OUNCE) CAN EVAPORATED MILK, ROOM TEMPERATURE

1 (14 OUNCE) CAN SWEETENED CONDENSED MILK, ROOM TEMPERATURE

Gently stir milks together until thoroughly combined. Carefully pour over cooled cake. Refrigerate.

CREAM ICING:

2 CUPS HEAVY CREAM

⅓ CUP SUGAR

SWEETENED, FLAKED COCONUT (OPTIONAL)

When ready to serve, beat together cream and sugar until stiff. Frost refrigerated cake and sprinkle with coconut if desired. Keep refrigerated.
Yield: 12 servings

PIES

Almond Pie

½ CUP BUTTER, MELTED

1 CUP SUGAR

3 EGGS, BEATEN

¾ CUP LIGHT CORN SYRUP

¼ TEASPOON SALT

1 TEASPOON VANILLA EXTRACT

2 CUPS CHOPPED ALMONDS

1 (9 INCH) PIE SHELL, UNBAKED

In a medium mixing bowl, combine butter, sugar, eggs, corn syrup, salt, and vanilla. Beat until well blended. Fold in almonds and pour into unbaked pie shell. Bake at 375° for 40 to 50 minutes or until set. Cool completely on a wire rack.
Yield: 8 servings

For a professional brown and shiny finish on your pastry, brush egg white onto the inside of your piecrust before filling it and on the top before baking.

Apple Crumble Pie

1 (9 INCH) DEEP-DISH PIE SHELL, UNBAKED

5 CUPS PEELED, THINLY SLICED APPLES (ABOUT 5 MEDIUM)

½ CUP SUGAR

¾ TEASPOON GROUND CINNAMON

⅓ CUP SUGAR

¾ CUP FLOUR

6 TABLESPOONS BUTTER

Arrange apple slices in unbaked pie shell. Mix ½ cup sugar with cinnamon; sprinkle over apples. Mix ⅓ cup sugar with flour; cut in butter until crumbly. Spoon mixture over apples. Bake at 400° for 35 to 40 minutes or until apples are soft and top is lightly browned.
Yield: 8 servings

Spend some time sharing your hopes and dreams for the coming year with your family. Then dedicate one evening each week during which you gather together to pray and ask the Lord's blessing on your family in the New Year.

If you believe, you will receive whatever you ask for in prayer.
MATTHEW 21:22

Applescotch Pie

5 CUPS PEELED, THINLY SLICED TART APPLES (ABOUT 5 MEDIUM)

1 CUP BROWN SUGAR, PACKED

¼ CUP WATER

1 TABLESPOON LEMON JUICE

¼ CUP FLOUR

2 TABLESPOONS SUGAR

¼ TEASPOON SALT

1 TEASPOON VANILLA EXTRACT

3 TABLESPOONS BUTTER OR MARGARINE

PASTRY FOR (9 INCH) DOUBLE-CRUST PIE

Combine apples, brown sugar, water, and lemon juice in a medium
saucepan. Cover and cook over medium heat until apples are tender, 5 to 10
minutes. Blend flour, sugar, and salt. Stir into apple mixture. Cook, stirring
constantly, until syrup thickens, about 2 minutes. Remove from heat; stir in
vanilla and butter. Pour into pastry-lined pie plate and cover with top crust;
slit to vent. Bake at 425° for 40 to 45 minutes.
Yield: 8 servings

Butterscotch Pie

1½ CUPS BROWN SUGAR

¼ TEASPOON SALT

2 TABLESPOONS FLOUR

3 TABLESPOONS CORNSTARCH

1½ CUPS HOT WATER

2 EGG YOLKS

1 TABLESPOON BUTTER

1 TEASPOON VANILLA EXTRACT

1 (9 INCH) PIE SHELL, BAKED

In a medium saucepan, mix together sugar, salt, flour, and cornstarch. Stir in hot water, blending well. Cook until thick and clear. Beat egg yolks. Add a small amount of hot mixture to egg yolks and mix well. Slowly blend egg yolks into hot sugar mixture, stirring constantly. Cook, stirring constantly, over low heat for 1 minute. Remove from heat and stir in butter and vanilla. Cool slightly, then pour into baked pie shell. Prepare meringue.

MERINGUE:

2 EGG WHITES

¼ TEASPOON CREAM OF TARTAR

½ TEASPOON VANILLA EXTRACT

4 TABLESPOONS SUGAR

Beat egg whites with cream of tartar and vanilla until soft peaks form. Add in sugar one tablespoon at a time, beating until stiff peaks form and sugar is dissolved. Spread meringue evenly over pie, sealing at pastry edges. Bake at 350° for 12 to 15 minutes or until meringue is golden. Let cool before serving.
Yield: 8 servings

Caramel Apple Pie

6 CUPS PEELED, THINLY SLICED TART APPLES (ABOUT 6 MEDIUM)

¾ CUP SUGAR

¼ CUP FLOUR

¼ TEASPOON SALT

PASTRY FOR DOUBLE-CRUST PIE, UNBAKED

2 TABLESPOONS BUTTER OR MARGARINE

⅓ CUP CARAMEL ICE CREAM TOPPING

4 TABLESPOONS CHOPPED PECANS

In a large bowl, combine apples, sugar, flour, and salt. Spoon apple mixture into pastry-lined pie pan. Dot with butter. Top with second pastry. Flute edges and cut slits in several places to let steam escape. Bake at 425° for 35 to 45 minutes or until apples are tender. Cover edge of piecrust with strip of foil during last 10 to 15 minutes of baking to prevent excessive browning. Remove pie from oven and immediately drizzle with caramel topping and sprinkle with pecans.
Yield: 8 servings

Caramel Pie

2 (14 OUNCE) CANS SWEETENED CONDENSED MILK

1 (9 INCH) PREPARED SHORTBREAD CRUST

1 (12 OUNCE) CARTON FROZEN WHIPPED TOPPING, THAWED

Remove labels from condensed milk cans. Place in a large pot and cover completely with water. Bring water to a boil over high heat; reduce heat to medium-high for 4 hours, adding water to keep cans covered. Remove cans from pot and cool slightly. Very carefully open cans and pour cooked milk into shortbread crust. Chill. Prior to serving, spread whipped topping evenly over pie.
Yield: 8 to 12 servings

Chocolate Pecan Pie

1½ CUPS COARSELY CHOPPED PECANS

1 CUP SEMISWEET CHOCOLATE CHIPS

1 (8 INCH) PIE SHELL, PARTIALLY BAKED

½ CUP LIGHT CORN SYRUP

½ CUP SUGAR

2 EGGS, LIGHTLY BEATEN

¼ CUP BUTTER, MELTED

Sprinkle pecans and chocolate chips into pie shell. In a mixing bowl, combine corn syrup, sugar, eggs, and butter. Mix well. Slowly pour mixture over pecans and chocolate. Bake at 325° for 1 hour.
Yield: 8 to 12 servings

To protect the edges of your piecrust from overbrowning, grab a disposable aluminum pie pan. Cut out the bottom of the pan. The ring is perfect for setting down over your baking pie during the last fourth of baking time.

Christmas Angel Pie

1 CAN SWEETENED CONDENSED MILK

⅓ CUP LEMON JUICE

1 (10 OUNCE) PACKAGE FROZEN RASPBERRIES, THAWED AND DRAINED

½ PINT WHIPPING CREAM, WHIPPED

1 PREPARED GRAHAM CRACKER CRUMB OR SHORTBREAD CRUST

Stir together sweetened condensed milk and lemon juice. Fold in raspberries and whipping cream. Pour into graham cracker crust and chill. Yield: 8 servings

Classic Chess Pie

2 EGGS, BEATEN

1½ CUPS SUGAR

1 TABLESPOON FLOUR

1 TABLESPOON WHITE CORNMEAL

¼ CUP MILK

½ CUP BUTTER, MELTED

½ TEASPOON VANILLA EXTRACT

½ TEASPOON WHITE VINEGAR

1 (9 INCH) PIE SHELL, UNBAKED

In a mixing bowl, combine eggs with sugar, flour, and cornmeal. Add in milk, butter, vanilla, and vinegar. Pour into unbaked pie shell. Bake at 325° for 45 minutes. Decrease oven temperature to 300° and bake for an additional 10 minutes.
Yield: 8 servings

Coconut Cream Pie

⅔ CUP SUGAR

¼ CUP CORNSTARCH

½ TEASPOON SALT

3 CUPS MILK

4 EGG YOLKS, LIGHTLY BEATEN

2 TABLESPOONS BUTTER

2 TEASPOONS VANILLA EXTRACT

¾ CUP SWEETENED, FLAKED COCONUT

1 (9 INCH) PIE SHELL, BAKED

In a saucepan, mix sugar, cornstarch, and salt. Blend together milk and egg yolks and gradually stir into sugar mixture. Cook over medium heat, stirring constantly, until mixture is thickened and bubbly. Cook for 1 minute, stirring constantly; remove from heat. Stir in butter, vanilla, and coconut. Let cool slightly. Pour into baked pie shell and cover with plastic wrap. Chill pie thoroughly for at least 2 hours.

WHIPPED CREAM TOPPING:

1 CUP HEAVY CREAM, CHILLED

1 TEASPOON POWDERED SUGAR

¼ CUP SWEETENED, FLAKED COCONUT, TOASTED

Whip cream together with powdered sugar until stiff peaks form. Spread evenly over pie and sprinkle with toasted coconut.
Yield: 8 servings

Cranberry-Raisin Pie

1 CUP BROWN SUGAR

2 TABLESPOONS CORNSTARCH

2 CUPS RAISINS

½ TEASPOON GRATED ORANGE PEEL

½ CUP ORANGE JUICE

½ TEASPOON GRATED LEMON PEEL

2 TABLESPOONS LEMON JUICE

1⅓ CUPS COLD WATER

1 CUP CRANBERRIES

1 (9 INCH) PIE SHELL, UNBAKED, WITH PASTRY FOR LATTICE CRUST

Combine brown sugar and cornstarch in a saucepan. Stir in raisins, orange peel and juice, lemon peel and juice, and cold water. Cook and stir over medium heat until thick and bubbly. Cook for 1 minute, stirring constantly. Remove from heat and stir in cranberries. Let cool slightly; pour into unbaked pie shell. Top with lattice crust. Bake at 375° for 40 minutes. Yield: 8 servings

Step out in faith and trust God to provide for all your needs this Christmas. If your needs seem too great, remember that the Lord likes to surprise us in big ways. Talk to God; He's listening.

Double-Layer Pumpkin Pie

4 OUNCES CREAM CHEESE, SOFTENED

1 TABLESPOON COLD MILK

1 TABLESPOON SUGAR

1 (8 OUNCE) CARTON FROZEN WHIPPED TOPPING, THAWED AND DIVIDED

1 PREPARED GRAHAM CRACKER CRUMB CRUST

1 (16 OUNCE) CAN PUMPKIN

2 (4 SERVING SIZE) PACKAGES INSTANT VANILLA PUDDING

1 TEASPOON GROUND CINNAMON

½ TEASPOON GROUND GINGER

¼ TEASPOON GROUND CLOVES

1 CUP COLD MILK

In a large bowl, beat cream cheese, 1 tablespoon milk, and sugar until smooth. Gently stir in 1½ cups whipped topping. Spread on bottom of crust. In another bowl, whisk together pumpkin, pudding mix, spices, and 1 cup milk until well blended. Spread evenly over cream cheese layer. Refrigerate for at least 4 hours before serving. Serve with remaining whipped topping.

Yield: 8 servings

Double Pecan Pie

PECAN PASTRY:

1 CUP FLOUR

¼ CUP GROUND PECANS

¼ TEASPOON SALT

¼ CUP PLUS 2 TABLESPOONS
BUTTER OR MARGARINE

1 TO 2 TABLESPOONS COLD WATER

PIE FILLING:

1 CUP LIGHT CORN SYRUP

¾ CUP SUGAR

3 EGGS, BEATEN

3 TABLESPOONS BUTTER OR
MARGARINE, MELTED

2 TEASPOONS VANILLA EXTRACT

¼ TEASPOON SALT

1 CUP PECAN PIECES

1 CUP PECAN HALVES

Prepare pecan pastry by combining flour, pecans, and salt in a medium bowl; cut in butter with a pastry blender until mixture resembles coarse meal. Sprinkle water over mixture, stirring just until dry ingredients are moistened. Shape pastry into a ball and chill for 30 minutes. On a floured surface, roll pastry to ⅛-inch thickness. Place in a 9-inch pie pan and flute edges. Set aside.

In a medium mixing bowl, combine corn syrup, sugar, eggs, butter, vanilla, and salt. Beat at medium speed just until blended. Stir in pecan pieces. Pour mixture into pecan pastry. Top with pecan halves. Bake at 350° for 50 to 60 minutes or until set. If edges begin to brown excessively, cover edges with aluminum foil.
Yield: 8 to 12 servings

Finger Pecan Tarts

PASTRY:

3 OUNCES CREAM CHEESE

½ CUP BUTTER (NO SUBSTITUTIONS)

1 CUP FLOUR

Mix cream cheese, butter, and flour together with a pastry blender. Roll into 24 balls (the size of large marbles) and press into mini muffin tins.

FILLING:

1½ CUPS BROWN SUGAR

2 TABLESPOONS BUTTER, MELTED

1 PINCH SALT

1 TEASPOON VANILLA EXTRACT

2 EGGS, SLIGHTLY BEATEN

1 CUP CHOPPED PECANS

In a pitcher, blend together sugar, butter, salt, vanilla, and eggs; pour into pastry shells and top with pecans. Bake at 350° for 20 minutes or until crusts turn golden and centers are firm.
Yield: 24 tarts

Old metal racks from worn-out refrigerators and ovens make good cooling racks for cookies and other baked goods. Their large size is great for holiday baking sprees.

French Silk Pie

1 CUP SUGAR

¾ CUP BUTTER (NO SUBSTITUTIONS)

**3 SQUARES (1 OUNCE EACH) UNSWEETENED CHOCOLATE,
MELTED AND COOLED**

1½ TEASPOONS VANILLA EXTRACT

¾ CUP EGG SUBSTITUTE

1 (9 INCH) PIE SHELL, BAKED

In a mixing bowl, cream together sugar and butter until light and fluffy. Blend in chocolate and vanilla. Slowly add egg substitute, ¼ cup at a time, beating for 2 to 3 minutes after each addition and scraping sides of bowl frequently. Pour into baked pie shell and chill thoroughly.
Yield: 6 to 8 servings

*Whatever you give to others this Christmas,
be sure to give from your heart.*

Fudge Brownie Nut Pie

1 (14 OUNCE) CAN SWEETENED CONDENSED MILK

½ CUP COCOA

¼ CUP BUTTER OR MARGARINE

1 CUP FLOUR

3 LARGE EGGS, BEATEN

1 TEASPOON VANILLA EXTRACT

1¾ CUPS CHOPPED PECANS

1 (9 INCH) PIE SHELL, UNBAKED

In a medium saucepan over low heat, stir together milk, cocoa, and butter. When butter melts and mixture is heated through, remove from heat. Stir in flour, eggs, vanilla, and pecans; pour into pie shell. Bake at 350° for 50 minutes or until center is set.

Yield: 8 servings

Holiday Apple Pie

3 CUPS PEELED, THINLY SLICED BAKING APPLES

1 (16 OUNCE) CAN WHOLE-BERRY CRANBERRY SAUCE

¾ CUP CHOPPED WALNUTS

½ CUP SUGAR

¼ CUP FLOUR

1 TEASPOON GROUND CINNAMON

PASTRY FOR 1 (9 INCH) DOUBLE-CRUST PIE

In a large bowl, combine apples, cranberry sauce, walnuts, sugar, flour, and cinnamon; toss until evenly coated. Pour into pastry pie plate; top with pie dough rolled to ⅛-inch thickness. Flute edges and cut slits in top crust to allow steam to escape. Place on a baking sheet and bake at 375° for 40 to 45 minutes or until lightly browned.
Yield: 8 servings

Lemon Chess Pie

4 EGGS, LIGHTLY WHISKED

1½ CUPS SUGAR

2 TABLESPOONS WHITE CORNMEAL

¼ CUP BUTTER, MELTED

½ CUP MILK

2 LEMONS, JUICED

1 (9 INCH) PIE SHELL, UNBAKED

In a large mixing bowl, combine eggs, sugar, cornmeal, melted butter, milk, and lemon juice. Stir to dissolve sugar completely. Pour filling into unbaked pie shell. Bake at 425° for 10 minutes; then reduce temperature to 350° and continue to bake until set, approximately 25 minutes. Serve at room temperature.
Yield: 8 servings

Melt-in-Your-Mouth Pie

1 (14 OUNCE) CAN SWEETENED CONDENSED MILK

⅓ CUP LEMON JUICE

⅓ CUP FLAKED COCONUT

⅓ CUP CHOPPED PECANS

1 (8 OUNCE) CAN CRUSHED PINEAPPLE, DRAINED

1 (12 OUNCE) CARTON FROZEN WHIPPED TOPPING, THAWED

1 (9 INCH) PREPARED GRAHAM CRACKER CRUMB CRUST

In a mixing bowl, combine sweetened condensed milk and lemon juice. Gently stir in coconut, pecans, and pineapple. Fold in whipped topping. Spoon into prepared crust. Refrigerate for several hours before serving. Yield: 8 servings

Old-Fashioned Chocolate Meringue Pie

¾ CUP SUGAR

5 TABLESPOONS COCOA

3 TABLESPOONS CORNSTARCH

¼ TEASPOON SALT

2 CUPS MILK

3 EGG YOLKS, BEATEN

1 TEASPOON VANILLA EXTRACT

1 (9 INCH) PIE SHELL, BAKED

MERINGUE:

3 EGG WHITES

½ TEASPOON CREAM OF TARTAR

6 TABLESPOONS SUGAR

In a heavy saucepan, mix sugar, cocoa, cornstarch, and salt. Gradually stir in milk. Cook and stir over medium-high heat until thickened and bubbly. Reduce heat and cook for 2 more minutes, stirring constantly. Remove from heat. Stir approximately 1 cup of hot mixture into egg yolks. Return to saucepan and bring to a gentle boil. Cook and stir for 2 minutes. Remove from heat and stir in vanilla. Pour hot filling into pie shell. Set aside and prepare meringue. In a cold mixing bowl, beat egg whites and cream of tartar until soft peaks form. Gradually beat in sugar. Continue to beat until stiff, glossy peaks form. Spread evenly over hot pie filling, being sure to seal edges. Bake at 350° for 12 to 15 minutes or until meringue is golden. Yield: 8 servings

Peanut Butter Pie

1 (8 OUNCE) PACKAGE CREAM CHEESE, SOFTENED

⅔ CUP CREAMY PEANUT BUTTER

1 (14 OUNCE) CAN SWEETENED CONDENSED MILK

1 (8 OUNCE) CARTON FROZEN WHIPPED TOPPING, THAWED

1 PREPARED GRAHAM CRACKER CRUMB CRUST

Beat cream cheese, peanut butter, and sweetened condensed milk together until smooth. Fold in whipped topping. Spoon into graham cracker crust. Chill.
Yield: 8 servings

Quick Chocolate Bar Pie

1 (7 OUNCE) MILK CHOCOLATE BAR, DIVIDED

2 TABLESPOONS MILK

1 (8 OUNCE) CARTON FROZEN WHIPPED TOPPING, THAWED AND DIVIDED

1 (9 INCH) PIE SHELL, BAKED

Melt chocolate bar, minus 3 squares, in a bowl placed over hot (not boiling) water. Gradually stir in milk. Cool slightly; then fold in whipped topping. Blend well; pour into prepared pie shell. Grate or shave remaining chocolate over pie. Chill.
Yield: 8 servings

Sour Cream Pear Pie

4 CUPS PEELED, SLICED PEARS

⅓ CUP SUGAR

2 TABLESPOONS FLOUR

1 (8 OUNCE) CARTON SOUR CREAM

1 TEASPOON VANILLA EXTRACT

½ TEASPOON ALMOND EXTRACT

1 (9 INCH) PIE SHELL, UNBAKED

TOPPING:

¼ CUP FLOUR

2 TABLESPOONS BUTTER OR MARGARINE, MELTED

2 TABLESPOONS BROWN SUGAR

In a large mixing bowl, toss pears with sugar and flour. Mix in sour cream, vanilla, and almond extract. Blend well and pour into unbaked pie shell. In a small bowl, mix flour, butter, and brown sugar until crumbly. Sprinkle mixture over pears. Bake at 400° for 10 minutes; then reduce temperature to 350° and bake for 45 minutes or until pears are tender.
Yield: 6 to 8 servings

Traditional Pumpkin Pie

1 (15 OUNCE) CAN PUMPKIN

1 (14 OUNCE) CAN SWEETENED CONDENSED MILK

2 EGGS, LIGHTLY BEATEN

1 TEASPOON GROUND CINNAMON

½ TEASPOON GROUND GINGER

½ TEASPOON GROUND NUTMEG

¼ TEASPOON GROUND CLOVES

½ TEASPOON SALT

1 (9 INCH) PIE SHELL, UNBAKED

Whisk pumpkin, milk, eggs, spices, and salt in a medium bowl until smooth. Pour into unbaked pie shell. Bake at 425° for 15 minutes; then reduce oven temperature to 350° and continue baking for 35 to 40 minutes or until knife inserted 1 inch from crust comes out clean. Cool.
Yield: 8 servings

Add a little happy to your holiday. When you find yourself feeling overly stressed this Christmas, curl up in your favorite chair with a steaming mug of coffee and a slice of pumpkin pie (don't forget loads of whipped topping!) and read through your favorite portion of scripture. You'll be more joyful for it!

Tropical Peach Pie

1 CUP BROWN SUGAR, PACKED

¼ CUP BUTTER OR MARGARINE

½ CUP FLOUR

½ TEASPOON GROUND CINNAMON

⅛ TEASPOON SALT

1 (9 INCH) PIE SHELL, BAKED

1 LARGE CAN SLICED PEACHES, DRAINED

1 CUP CRUSHED PINEAPPLE, DRAINED

¼ CUP WHIPPING CREAM

Cream brown sugar and butter. Stir in flour, cinnamon, and salt. Sprinkle half of mixture in baked pie shell. Cover with peaches. Top with crushed pineapple. Pour cream over all. Sprinkle remaining sugar mixture on top. Bake at 400° for 15 minutes. Reduce heat to 350° and bake 40 to 45 minutes longer.
Yield: 8 servings

Holiday Goodies Cheat Sheets

CANDY COOKING TERMINOLOGY

THREAD—230°—Candy will create a thin thread or ribbon when dropped from a spoon. (Syrup)

SOFT BALL—234°—When dropped into water, candy will form a ball that is moldable when handled. (Fudge)

FIRM BALL—244°—This ball will hold a good shape but flatten when pressed. (Caramel)

HARD BALL—250°—At this point the ball is very firm, sticky. (Rock candy)

SOFT CRACK—270°—The ball will stretch into hard but not brittle threads. (Taffy)

HARD CRACK—300°—Tap this ball against something, and it will break into brittle pieces. (Peanut brittle)

EQUIVALENT PAN SIZES

Use two 8-inch layer pans or 1½ to 2 dozen cupcakes in muffin tins.

Use three 8-inch layer pans or two 9-inch square pans.

Use one 9-inch layer pan or one 8-inch square pan.

Use two 9-inch layer pans or one 9 x 13 inch pan or one 9-inch tube pan or two 8-inch square pans.

Use one 5 x 9 inch loaf pan or two dozen cupcakes in muffin tins.

Index

Also Available from Mary & Martha...

In the Kitchen with Mary & Martha is not your ordinary cookbook. With two lovable characters, oodles of kitchen tips and heartfelt inspiration, and an overabundance of recipes for delicious dishes (all of which have received the Mary & Martha Stamp of Approval), this delightful volume is the first in a must-have series for cooks of all ages. The hardback, comb-bound cookbook includes recipes for family favorites—like those gooey cookies Grandma used to make!—and includes adorable illustrations and two-color ink throughout. A guaranteed-to-please package makes this a great gift.

ISBN 1-59310-878-8 / $14.97 U.S.

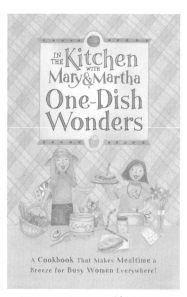

ISBN 1-59789-011-1 / $14.97 U.S.

This must-have cookbook for busy women features 200 recipes for entire meals, snacks, and dinner additions that are guaranteed to simplify meal preparation—and cleanup, too. And, as always, each recipe carries the Mary & Martha Stamp of Approval. Mary & Martha also offer up old-fashioned family inspiration and absolutely amazing time-saving kitchen tips. As if that isn't enough, this hardback, comb-bound book includes adorable illustrations and two-color ink throughout. At only $14.97, busy women will have a hard time passing this one up!

Available Wherever Books Are Sold